A Study Guide for the New Edexcel IGCSE Anthology Poetry for the Literature Exam:

A Line by Line Analysis of all the Poems with Exam Tips for Success

Josephine Pearce

A Study Smart Guide

1.If by Rudyard Kipling

2.Prayer Before Birth by Louis MacNeice

3.Blessing by Imtiaz Dharker

4.Search for my Tongue by Sujata Bhatt

5.Half-past Two by U.A. Fanthorpe

6.Piano by D.H. Lawrence

7.Hide and Seek by Vernon Scannell

8.Sonnet 116 by William Shakespeare

9.La Belle Dame Sans Merci by John Keats

10.Poem at Thirty Nine by Alice Walker

11.War Photographer by Carol Ann Duffy

12.The Tyger by William Blake

13.My Last Duchess by Robert Browning

14.Half-caste by John Agard

15.Do not go gentle into that good night by Dylan Thomas

16.Remember by Christina Rossetti

Edexcel

International GCSE in English Literature

Paper 1 Poetry and Modern Prose

Paper 1: Poetry and Modern Prose

Exam worth 60% of entire Literature GCSE

Content of Exam

Section A: Essay on an unseen poem

Section B: Essay comparing two poems from the Anthology Poetry

Section C: Essay on a modern prose text

This book is a guide to all the poems you could be tested on in Section B of the Literature exam.

Each poem has a line by line analysis of techniques and meanings, followed by suggestions for other poems with which to compare it in the exam.

1. "If" by Rudyard Kipling

POET

Rudyard Kipling (1865-1936)

Rudyard Kipling is a famous English short story writer who also wrote poetry. His most famous work is "The Jungle Book". He was highly acclaimed and celebrated during his own lifetime, winning the Nobel Prize for literature in 1907.

He was born in Bombay in India where his father was a professor at the School of Art. Although Kipling went to school in England, he returned to Lahore, where his father had become the curator of the museum, when he was 16. Kipling became assistant editor of a small local newspaper, the "Civil and Military Gazette". In his role as a journalist, Kipling gained knowledge of the lives of the Indians and the British living abroad. He turned these experiences into many short stories and novels.

When his writing took off, Kipling left India to return to London and devote his time to fiction. He married and travelled to America where he met other famous writers. He eventually settled with his family in Devon, England, where he wrote prolifically.

BACKGROUND

The poem was first published in 1910 and is addressed to Kipling's son, John. Kipling's son died in 1915 at the Battle of Loos during the First World War. He was just eighteen years old.

The poem was inspired by Kipling's admiration for Leander Starr Jameson. Jameson was a Scottish politician who fought to colonise Africa. He led an infamous uprising, called the Jameson raid, in which he tried to gather British expatriate workers in South Africa to fight against the Boer (or Dutch-speaking) population which ran the country. The raid failed and Jameson was arrested and put on trial in South Africa. Back home in England, the press and the people hailed him as a hero for trying to snatch the country back from the Boers. Jameson was sent to prison for 15 months. Upon his release, he became Prime Minister of Cape Colony in South Africa.

Kipling was introduced to Jameson by his friend Cecil Rhodes. Rhodes was a British businessman who had founded the country of Rhodesia in southern Africa. Rhodes colonised this African territory, exploiting its natural resources and making himself a very wealthy man. Rhodesia has now been returned to its indigenous people and is Zimbabwe and Zambia. Kipling was a great believer in British Empire. This was the political practice of the British taking over territories abroad, governing their peoples, and taking their wealth and resources. By 1922, the British Empire was made up of 458 million people, and covered a quarter of the planet. It made Britain very wealthy and powerful.

The poem is inspired by the activities of men like Jameson whom Kipling felt encapsulated what it means to be a British man. The qualities he prizes most in the poem are humility or not being boastful, and stoicism or enduring hardship without making a fuss.

SUMMARY

The poem is a father's advice to his son on how to be a great British man.

ANALYSIS

The poem is a direct address from a father to his son, explaining the qualities which will make the boy a fine man. It is written in the second person, like an instruction manual, speaking to "you" Kipling's son and the reader. Explicitly, the poem is Kipling's words to his son, John. However, it was inspired by Kipling's friend Leander Starr Jameson.

The poem is structured as one long sentence with every line flowing on to the next. This perpetual enjambment creates a sense of pace, urgency and dynamism. This gives the poem the feeling that something important is being said which must be heard. The poem is didactic. This means that it is meant to instruct and educate. Kipling is trying to educate his son, and also the reader, to recognise and aspire to becoming a British gentleman. The poem is constructed around four stanzas, each with eight lines. There is an organised rhyme scheme of ABABCDCD which again gives the poem great pace and direction.

The poem is entitled "If". The word "If" at the beginning of a sentence forms a conditional. Conditional sentences describe known facts and their consequences. The poem is therefore a list of statements which pose a series of conditions or circumstances. The consequence of those circumstances is held back until the final line of the entire poem. This gives the poem a sense of drama and anticipation. The reader is waiting to find out what will be the consequence if they behave in the way described by the poet. The final line of the poem builds to the crescendo that the individual who can fulfil all these circumstances will be a "Man".

The first stanza begins with the word "If". The word forms a refrain throughout the poem, being repeated at the beginning of most lines. Because the word "if" here begs the question 'is it possible', its repetition keeps forcing the reader to think about whether or not they can live up to the circumstances or conditions described in the poem. It sets us a challenge which we feel we should meet.

The first stanza begins with a metaphor of calm. The image "keep your head" suggests that real men are able not to lose control and panic, losing your head means becoming out of rational control. The poet explains that a man must not only be calm every day, he must especially be calm when others are "losing" their heads and "blaming it on you". Immediately, the reader is given a picture of a calm and able man who is not flustered by others panicking and who has broad enough shoulders not to care if others try to shift responsibility on to him.

The poet goes on to explain that you are a man "If you can trust yourself when all men doubt you". This captures the idea of self-belief. Kipling is saying that a real man always sticks with his own judgement and is confident in his abilities. However, this man does not care if others doubt him. Instead he makes "allowance" or excuses for those around him too foolish to appreciate him.

The next circumstance which makes you a man is being able to "wait and not be tired" and to avoid lying when others lie about you, and avoid hating when others hate you. In the final line of the stanza, Kipling says a real man should not "look too good, nor talk too wise". This is interesting. He is suggesting that the model of masculinity does not show off to others or try to impress. This quiet stoicism is part of the stereotype of the British gentleman who has a 'stiff upper lip'. This means that he does not complain even when things go badly for him.

8

The second stanza moves on from the times when things go wrong, to thoughts of ambition. It begins with the conditional idea "If you can dream – and not make dreams your master". Here the idea of dreams means ambitions and aspirations. It is suggesting that ambition is an important thing. However, the poet does not think a real man ever loses control, so he does not allow ambition to drive him. Kipling imagines the dreams as a person becoming the boss or "master"; a real man would never allow this to happen. He goes on to say that men should be able to "think – and not make thoughts your aim". This is very telling. Kipling is saying that thoughts are vital, but they should not be your only goal. He believes that actions and doing things are more important than thinking. Again this is part of the model of practical masculinity which formed the basis of the British Empire.

Kipling goes on to explain that while a real man is ambitious, he must know how to deal with failure. He says that it is vital to "meet with Triumph and Disaster…just the same". Here he personifies success and failure and imagines a meeting with them. He says that you must learn to greet each of them in the same way. Therefore you will be as unfazed by success as you are by failure. You will take it all in your stride. Interestingly, Kipling calls success and failure "two impostors". An impostor is someone who pretends to be someone they are not in order to deceive you. Kipling is highlighting the way that success and failure are never really what you think they are; they both have hidden drawbacks which mean that we should neither be too excited or too disappointed by outcomes.

The poet goes on to imagine the sort of determination one must have to listen to your own words being "twisted by knaves". A knave is an old-fashioned or archaic name for a dishonest person. Kipling concludes the stanza by explaining that determination must be shown when a man watches the "things you gave your life to, broken". In this circumstance a man will "build 'em up with worn-out tools". This is a metaphor comparing success with building something and failure with the destruction of that building. He imagines a real man as a builder who is prepared to return to a broken house and begin again without complaining if disaster hits. Again, Kipling's imagery is practical and masculine. It is about making something.

Stanza three moves on to ideas of taking risks and being daring which are part of Kipling's stereotype of masculinity. The first metaphor comes from gambling. He imagines a man able to risk his life being like a gambler willing to "heap" his winnings "And risk it on one turn of pitch-and-toss". This is a gambling game of luck. Therefore a man will be prepared to risk his life for the toss of a coin. However, Kipling's point continues. It is not just the risk which is manly, it is the ability to deal with loss and never "breathe a word about" it which is important. This shows stoicism and a sense of proportion. The poet goes on to imagine other dangerous situations a man might face. He states a man must be able to "force your heart and nerve and sinew". The polysyndeton or repeated use of "and" to connect the list here emphasizes all the details necessary to make a man. Importantly, a man is made not only of heart, meaning emotion, but also of "nerve" which is associated with bravery, and "sinew" which means muscle and implies physical power. It is these qualities which a man must have when all others have given up. A real man remains because his "Will which says to them: 'Hold on!'" Thus a man has a greater "Will" or sense of sheer determination which will make him persist when others give up.

In the final stanza, Kipling deals with the way a man should have relationships with others. He begins by saying that a man must "talk with crowds and keep your virtue". This means a man must be able to speak to the masses but not be influenced by their poor behaviour. It assumes that ordinary people are not as virtuous or moral as a real man. Kipling then says a man must "walk with Kings – nor lose the common touch". Therefore a great man knows how to speak to kings and still be a normal person; he must not become too arrogant or superior because of the elevated people he knows.

Kipling goes on to say that a man should not be able to be "hurt" by "foes nor loving friends". This suggests that a man is impervious to emotional pain caused by enemies and lovers. This means a man must not have a deep emotional investment in others. Kipling develops this idea of being emotionally cut off when he says "If all men count with you, but none too much". This means you should pay equal attention to individuals and never favour one person over another. The word "count" comes from mathematics and suggests that a man measures others equally. This is a very rational way of dealing with individuals.

Now the poet moves on to building to the conclusion of his point. He introduces a clever metaphor for life as a journey of one minute. The "unforgiving minute" is the length of time that life feels like. It is brief and it is "unforgiving" because it will not give you a second more or less even if you beg for it. Therefore life is short. In this brief life a real man will fill his minute with "sixty seconds worth of distance". In other words, he will use up all his time on earth by running forward and doing things; he will never stop or idle. This shows that a man must seize his life and make the most of it.

Kipling explains that if his son can do all the things he has just listed then "Yours is the Earth and everything that's in it". Therefore with these qualities a man can look forward to owning the world; he can be a master of his planet. The character traits Kipling has just taught will lead to worldly success.

The final line begins with "And". This is a conjunction which should join two sentences together. Here it joins all the circumstances listed in the poem to the final fact that is their consequence – that they will make a boy a man. Importantly, Kipling uses the phrase "which is more". This means he thinks mastering the world is less important than the fact his boy will be a "Man". The word man is given a capital letter to show that it is a crucial concept. It is an important quality in itself and not just a gender.

The poem ends with the very personal phrase "my son!" This brings us back to the fact that this is fatherly advice meant for his son that we are eavesdropping on. The exclamation mark which ends the entire sentence of the poem shows the emotion which the poet has expressed here. He is triumphant and excited that his son is going to be a great man.

POEMS WITH LOTS OF POTENTIAL COMPARISONS WITH THIS ONE

"Prayer Before Birth" – provides useful comparisons with the poem as they are both about a cruel world. However, Kipling sees it as brave and admirable to face it, while MacNeice suggests it is better not to encounter life at all.

"Search for my Tongue" – provides useful comparisons as both poems are about what makes a person who they are.

"Piano" – provides useful comparisons. Both poems are about a son's relationship with a parent.

"Poem at Thirty Nine" – provides useful comparisons. Both poems are about a parent-child relationship which has been very influential.

"Do not go gentle into that good night" – provides useful comparisons as it is about the advice a son gives to his father. It is therefore the reverse of Kipling's poem.

POET

Louis MacNeice (1907-1963)

MacNeice was an Irish poet and playwright. His father was a Protestant minister and later a bishop of the Anglican Church of Ireland. He attended Oxford University where he met W.H. Auden and began publishing poetry as an undergraduate. He was part of the Auden Group of poets writing in the 1930s which included W.H. Auden, Stephen Spender and Cecil Day-Lewis. He was critically-acclaimed during his own lifetime. He spent World War II working for the BBC writing and producing radio programmes intended to create support for Britain's allies in the conflict. His poetry focuses on both the importance of human kindness in the face of totalitarian regimes, and the significance of Ireland.

MacNeice wrote in the introduction to his "Autumnal Journal": "Poetry in my opinion must be honest before anything else."

BACKGROUND

The poem was written at the end of World War II, 1944, after a period of prolonged bombing in London. It encapsulates the fear the nation felt for the future.

SUMMARY

The poem is spoken by an unborn foetus. The child pleads to the world into which it is about to come to be kind to it and not mistreat it. The baby concludes that if mankind cannot guarantee his wellbeing then he would rather be killed before being born.

ANALYSIS

The poem is a dramatic monologue spoken by an unborn child. The sex of the child is not specified which makes it universal and relatable to all readers.

The word "prayer" in the title suggests that the foetus needs to pray or appeal for help even from the womb. It is shocking to the reader that an unborn child might have any troubles or concerns; most readers would perceive a foetus as an innocent entity. This suggests that the world the child is about to enter must be terrifying and brutal. The word "prayer" is also part of the religious diction of the poem. This is employed ironically as there does not seem to be a god or moral force in the world which is described for the child to pray to.

The poem is written in free verse, with no set rhyme scheme or rhythm. This echoes the sense of randomness in the world which the baby fears. The brutality of the universe into which the child is going to be born is also made explicit in the ragged edges of the stanzas. They are jagged and violent looking.

The first stanza begins with a personal pronoun, "I". The rest of the poem also contains many personal pronouns, especially the word "me". The repetition of these pronouns creates a strong sense of the child's individual voice speaking. It also creates the impression of intense personal concern and anxiety.

The opening line is an imperative with an exclamatory word, "O hear me." The exclamation "O" communicates the intense anxiety of the speaker. The sentence is also an instruction to be heard. The implication is that there is some force out there which will hear the child, but it is not clear if it is a god, God or mankind. Notice the voice speaks the entire poem without receiving an answer. This suggests that God may not listen or exist and that humanity does not care about the child.

Phrases like "Let not" echo the Biblical grammar of the Old Testament, such as the Ten Commandments. The expression reminds the reader of the seriousness of the child's appeal. The baby wants to protected from the "bloodsucking bat or the rat or the stoat or the club-footed ghoul". The list is made to seem anxious through the repetition of "or the" which keeps adding on more things of which to be afraid. There is also alliteration on "bloodsucking bat" and assonance in "bat", "rat" and "stoat". These echoes create a sense of excess and a pace to the list. The images of the vampire bat and the monster from a scary film show the child is afraid of traditional forms of horror. However, as the poem progresses, we see that these are the least of the child's concerns; mankind is more horrific than fiction and myth.

The second stanza echoes the first verse, creating a refrain with the line "I am not yet born" which is repeated at the start of all the stanzas apart from the final one. This gives the poem a structure as well as the suggestion that if the child's appeal does not change throughout then no one is listening to it.

In the second stanza, the foetus wants someone to "console me". This means to provide comfort. The suggestion is that babies are not comforted or supported by grownups. The baby goes on to explain that it fears humans will "wall me", "dope me", "lure me" and "roll me". The repeated verbs emphasize strongly the things the child is afraid of. The human cruelties include oppressing, creating addiction, manipulating with lies, and submerging in torture instruments. The "black racks" and "blood baths" are a terrible vision of man's cruelty to fellow man.

In stanza three, the baby moves on to asking for things – "provide me". Interestingly, the things the baby wants are personified – water to "dandle me", "sky to sing to me". This suggests that nature is more maternal and kind than human beings. It shows that humans are out of step with the natural world and are crueller than it. The "white light" may be a moral sense which the child thinks it cannot learn from humans and can only find through untouched nature.

In stanza four, the child begs "forgive me". It explains that as all humans do cruel, sinful things, therefore it will not be able to prevent itself from also doing them when it is born. It is asking to be forgiven for the things it will inevitably do in the future, just by virtue of being human. This implies that mankind is inescapably cruel. The sins the child fears and expects to commit include cruel words and thoughts, as well as betrayal and murder. These acts are not only the child's responsibility. The stanza repeats the pronoun "they" four times, suggesting there is a faceless force or authority which coerces men to do evil.

In stanza five, the child asks to "rehearse me". This means to learn how to act. The suggestion is that in life people play "parts" and cannot be honest and true to themselves. The baby realises it must learn how to respond to a list of different types of people who will turn against him. He describes an unfriendly universe where "lovers laugh at me" and "my children curse me".

Stanza six begins a deterioration of the verse form as the stanzas become more randomly structured. This shows either the breakdown of modern society or the increasing pace of the terror which will lead to a crescendo of horror in the final line. This stanza repeats the first stanza, showing no one is listening the baby. Indeed the anxiety of the foetus has only increased since the opening of the poem as now the child says that man "is beast" or animal and he "thinks he is God". This suggests a power-crazed and brutal society where there is no higher moral guidance. Worse still, the baby now pleads for someone to prevent man ever coming "near me". The baby ironically despises mankind even though he will soon be part of it.

Stanza seven, finds the baby begging to be filled up with "strength" to prevent the dehumanising aspects of modern life. This is the opposite of stanza three where nature was personified as providing care for the baby. Here the baby fears that he will be turned into a "lethal automaton". This is a robot which kills. It is not clear if the robot kills others or destroys the baby who becomes it. Both interpretations are horrifying. The metaphor "a cog in a machine" is also used which suggests the child will be part of something beyond its control which exploits the baby. This loss of free will is a source of terror. The baby repeats the word "thing" in the stanza to show he fears becoming not human. Finally, the baby dreads being treated carelessly. He uses two similes. The first is "like thistledown" and then "like water". Both these natural products are delicate and easily lost. He imagines himself blown around or spilt. The child fears being turned into a machine or having his individuality lost.

The final stanza is made of two lines; each one is a separate sentence. This gives the verse a sense of climax and finality. This is the culmination of the horror which the child dreads; it could be a simple crescendo or a moment of explosion. The child once again uses Biblical grammar – "Let them not". He is still appealing to a listener which has not responded. The baby describes his fear with two related metaphors. First, the child does not want to be made "a stone". The metaphor suggests a hardening and deadening of human emotion. Secondly, the child begs "let them not spill me". Here he imagines himself as a liquid, possibly water which is usually held to be the opposite of stone. The water is dealt with carelessly and allowed to escape and be lost. Therefore the child is afraid of being misused without thought or compassion. The last line of the poem is an incomplete sentence – "Otherwise kill me." This makes it seem even more abrupt and anxious. The child offers an alternative to being born into this horror. The baby asks to be killed rather than made evil and exploited by mankind. The shock that an unborn child might want to die is profound. The reader is left with a powerful image of the way new life rejects the modern world and would rather not exist within it.

POEMS WITH LOTS OF POTENTIAL COMPARISONS WITH THIS ONE

"Half Past Two" – provides an alternative child's point of view. The speaker has also been neglected by grownups.

"Hide and Seek" – provides another portrait of cruelty and lack of compassion towards children. This time the cruelty is meted out by other children.

"Poem at Thirty Nine" – provides a contrasting style of personal address to the reader about an individual becoming a person they can be proud of. This is a strong contrast to MacNeice's poem where the baby would be ashamed to be human.

3. "Blessing" by Imtiaz Dharker

POET

Imtiaz Dharker (1954-Present)

Imtiaz Dharker was born in Lahore, Pakistan, to Pakistani parents. When she was less than a year old, her parents moved to Glasgow where she was brought up. She writes poetry, as well as producing documentaries and films. She now lives in both Britain and Mumbai, India, feeling a strong affinity with both countries and cultures.

She has won the Queen's Gold Medal for her English poetry.

BACKGROUND

The poem describes the dry season in India when temperatures reach 40 degrees centigrade and there is no rain. At these times, the people who live in the slums of Mumbai suffer terribly from a lack of water. Dharker's poem describes events in the slums during a drought when a water pipe bursts.

SUMMARY

The poem is a celebration of the life-giving power of water. It describes in religious terms the miracle that water can bring to the poor living in the slums of Mumbai. At the beginning of the poem there is no water. It is a time of drought. However, when a pipe bursts, the children collect the gushing water and their bodies become glittering and perfect with the blessing of God.

ANALYSIS

The title of the poem "Blessing" introduces the religious diction of the piece straight away. A blessing is something given by God. It is often a source of protection or kindness. It also has a secondary meaning of a prayer said before or after a meal. Both these meanings are present in Dharker's poem which shows us the generosity of God to bring the children water during a drought, as well as the fact the water is like a meal or feast for them after a time of deprivation.

The poem is written in free verse with no fixed rhyme or rhythm. However, the stanzas are cleverly constructed. At the beginning, when there is no water, the stanzas are short and brief. It is as though the words are dried up. But when the water erupts from the pipe, the stanzas become long and flowing. Indeed, stanzas three and four are connected by enjambment or a poetry line which runs the sentence on to the next verse. This flowing syntax imitates the flowing water gushing from the broken pipe.

In stanza one, Dharker describes what a lack of water looks like. She uses a simile comparing "The skin" to "a pod" or seed. "The skin" here could be the surface of the earth, the soil itself. According to this reading, "The skin" is a personification of the ground of India as it responds to the climate around it. A more obvious reading, is that the "skin" is the skin of the people of Mumbai. It describes how their skin becomes dehydrated during the Dry season; it becomes so dry it begins to crack. This splitting apart is compared with a seed "pod" which usually falls from a plant and opens out spilling its seed in order to start new

17

life. The image is therefore dehydrated, but it also shows the potential for a new beginning to come from it.

The second line of the stanza is another very short sentence. This structure of brief complete sentences as lines, imitates the lack of water and flowing goodness during the drought. This sentence sums up the situation the people have found themselves in – "There never is enough water". The word "never" emphasizes the constant lack of water which they experience. Cleverly, Dharker uses the word "water" only once in the poem. It is placed here at the beginning of the poem when there is not any. The word tells us what the poem is going to be about, but when the poet goes on to describe actual water she does not use the word again. Instead, she uses vivid descriptions to make us think about what water is really like.

Stanza two moves on to a powerful description of the beauty of water when you do not have it. It begins with the word "Imagine". This is an instruction or imperative to the reader, who is probably not lacking in water, to place themselves in the shoes of these people and empathize. We are asked to imagine "the drip of it". This prompts a sound memory of water which is underlined by the sibilance in the next line "small splash". The repeated 's' makes a pleasing flowing sound which resembles the noise of water moving. The fact the poem begins with a "drip" also creates a sense of pace. We start with no water, then we imagine a little, and finally we are treated to a description of lots of it cascading out.

Stanza two ends with a wonderful metaphor comparing the sound of water "in a tin mug" with "the voice of a kindly god". The reader can imagine the tinkling, bell-like sound water dripping on tin might make. This is then described as a voice; it is a personification. It is as though the water speaks to us. The voice is from a "kindly god". Here Dharker tells us that water is holy, or given by god. She makes us think about how precious and miraculous it is by imagining what it's like not to have any. Importantly, the god who speaks like water is "kindly", just as water itself is a benevolent element, bringing life to the world.

Stanza three moves us on to an event which happens in Mumbai, "Sometimes". This word underlines the rarity of this happening. It shows how special it is when it occurs. Dharker goes on to explain that occasionally there is "the sudden rush of fortune". This is a metaphor for the water pipe gushing. It compares the rupture to a "rush" or hurried outpouring of something. The moment the pipe bursts is a moment of "fortune". Here "fortune" means good luck. Therefore the breaking of the pipe, which some might see as an accident which needs to be repaired, is characterised as a great outpouring of luck.

Dharker explains that when the "municipal pipe bursts silver crashes to the ground". The water coming out of the pipe is described through a metaphor of treasure; it is like a precious metal, silver, cascading forth. Silver is a good image for water here as it has the same white shine to it as water. It is also a precious metal which is sometimes used to create coins or money. Dharker is showing that water is more valuable to these people than money, when they are thirsty and hot. The word "crashes" emphasizes the weight of the water flowing out. This makes it seem heavy and full; there is a lot of water.

The stanza runs on with lots of enjambment, creating a sense of the water flowing out. The poet continues "the flow has found a roar of tongues". The alliteration of the 'f' sound here underlines the rapid pace of the escaping water. There is then a metaphor comparing the voices of the people with the "roar" of an animal. The word "roar" suggests the people's

18

voices are not forming words; they are simply howling their appreciation for this miracle. "roar" also implies the loudness of the voices. They seem to be deafening. Finally, the "roar" brings the "tongues" of the people into one voice. Therefore they are united by this happy event of water in a hot, dry season.

The unifying nature of the water is emphasized by the continuing diction of religion on the next line. The people come as "a congregation". A "congregation" is a gathering of a community, usually in a church. Therefore the eruption of the pipe has brought together the people of the slum as one group ready to worship the god - water. In order to save the miracle of the water, the people dash to get containers for it, "pots, brass, copper, aluminium, plastic buckets". The eagerness with which the people try to collect the water is shown in the random objects they find to put it in. The stanza ends with an image of their haste as the people have "frantic hands". If something is "frantic" it is hurried, excited and disorganised. Dharker captures the happy chaos the water has caused.

The last sentence of stanza three runs on to stanza four. This enjambment imitates the flow of the water from the pipe. In the final stanza, Dharker describes the children enjoying the water and being transformed by it. The water is described as "liquid sun". This metaphor captures the shining brightness of the water. It shows how beautiful it is. The "naked children" play in the water and their skin, which began the poem dry and cracked "like a pod", is now "polished to perfection". The alliteration of the 'p' sound here emphasizes the harmony and glossiness which the water gives to the children's skin. They are shining in the "flashing light". The sun is sparkling off their wet bodies and creating flashes. Thus the water is miraculously transforming the children into jewels, sparkling.

These sight images of the water contrast the sound images from the beginning of the poem and affirm the way the element changes the people into something blessed and glowing. The final lines of the poem describe the gift God has given the children through the water – "as the blessing sings over their small bones". The water is "the blessing". Here "sings" is reminding us of the voice of the "kindly god" from the second stanza. The verb to sing also describes something positive and joyful which the water has brought to the children. Moreover singing is something congregations do in church to celebrate God. Therefore the water has brought about a moment of worship. The good fortune of the blessing plays across the "small bones" of the children. This final description shows the difference the water makes to the dried bodies of the people. It leaves the reader with a happy image of playing children who have been brought to life by the gift of water.

POEMS WITH LOTS OF POTENTIAL COMPARISONS WITH THIS ONE

"Prayer Before Birth" – provides a comparison between the anxieties of the unborn child about the world and the miraculous good fortune of these children who actually live in hardship.

"Hide and Seek" – provides interesting comparisons between the boy who is excluded by his community during the game, and the community which comes together here through the miracle of unexpected good fortune.

"War Photographer" – provides comparisons between the photographer who tries to raise awareness of the hardships people in other countries suffer, and the people of the slums who find a moment of happiness within that suffering.

"The Tyger" – provides comparisons between the poet wondering at the gifts God gives which are violent and dangerous, and the blessing given here of water in a time of drought.

4. "Search for my Tongue" by Sujata Bhatt

POET

Sujata Bhatt (1956-Present)

Bhatt was born in Gujarat, India, in 1956. In 1968, her family emigrated to America where she studied and lived most of her life. She is an accomplished poet who has received the Commonwealth Poetry Prize and the Cholmondeley Award for Poetry. She has translated Gujarati poetry by other writers into English. Much of her own poetry combines both the Gujarati and English languages. In 2013 she became the Visiting Professor of Creative Writing at Nottingham Trent University.

BACKGROUND

The extract is part of a longer poem which was inspired by her time studying English in America. She was concerned that her immersion in the English language might mean that she would lose her Indian identity.

Bhatt writes: "I have always thought of myself as an Indian who is outside India…That's the deepest layer of my identity."

SUMMARY

The poem voices the poet's anxiety that she is losing her mother tongue – Gujarati. She wonders if by living exclusively in one language, she will find her other voice will rot and die. However, she then dreams in Gujarati. These words are translated in the final section of the extract, where she expresses that her mother tongue cannot be destroyed.

ANALYSIS

The title of the poem, "Search for My Tongue", alludes to the colloquial phrase – mother tongue. The expression describes the language a person learns as a baby. It is a metaphor comparing a person's first language with a parent. It also describes the concept of language and communication through the physical embodiment of it – the tongue. Bhatt's title communicates her personal mission to find her true voice, and through that her true identity. Her confusion stems from the fact that she learnt Gujarati as a baby in India, but as a grownup now works and lives in an English-speaking world.

The poem is written in one long stanza. This gives a focus to her words, showing how important this issue is to her. The poem has no fixed rhythm or rhyme scheme; it is in free verse. The poem opens with the sentence, "You ask me what I mean by saying I have lost my tongue." This immediately identifies the speaker of the poem with the poet herself. This is a very personal poem. Moreover, the speaker seems to be engaged in a conversation which has been happening prior to the beginning of the extract. It appears the poet has already said that she feels she has "lost my tongue" and is now going to explain what she means. First, this suggests that her interlocutor, or the person to whom she is speaking, does not understand her. Secondly, this implies that she lives in a world which does not fully appreciate her situation and which requires her to explain herself.

The speaker goes on to turn the question back on to her interlocutor – "I ask you". Indeed the entire poem repeats the pronouns "you" and "your" a number of times. This makes the tone of the opening of the poem quite confrontational. The speaker of the poem is clearly feeling anxious, distressed and annoyed by the situation. She wants the person with whom she is speaking to understand how she feels. The reader is placed in the position of being the person who is being confronted with the poet's dilemma; we are made to face her problem and appreciate how she must feel.

In order to get this empathy, the poet asks "what would you do if you had two tongues in your mouth". Immediately, she is getting the interlocutor and the reader to imagine what it feels like to be her. This poem tries to create empathy for an experience that few people have; the experience of being bi-lingual or fluent in two languages. The image of "two tongues in your mouth" is striking and unpleasant. It makes the reader appreciate the sense of being too full up with words, almost choking on the languages.

The poet goes on to ask the reader to imagine how they would feel if they "lost the first one, the mother tongue". The use of the phrase "mother tongue" here emphasizes how personal and comforting the language of one's birth is. The idea of losing it seems horrifying. She goes on to explain that not only has she lost her original language, but she can "not really know the other, the foreign tongue". The word "foreign" here emphasizes the fact the poet feels that she does not belong in the English language. This is obviously surprising to the reader who is studying for a GCSE in the Language. It cleverly makes us think about what it would be like to feel these words did not fit with our own identity.

The poet continues in line eight with "You could not use them both together even if you thought that way". Here the poet explains her problem clearly. Having two languages is difficult because you cannot use them simultaneously. She cannot speak in both English and Gujarati at once; that would be gibberish. This reveals that every time she opens her mouth, she is forced to make a choice between her languages; she is made to prioritize one over the other, and she doesn't want to.

In line ten, the poet begins the sentence with "And". This is a conjunction which should be used to connect two parts of a sentence, not to introduce it. Here the word gives a sense of urgency to the poet's voice. She is running through her thoughts anxiously, so every sentence is connected to the next one because it is forming one larger expression of distress.

The poet again appeals to the reader to imagine what it feels like to be her, "And if you lived in a place you had to speak a foreign tongue". The word "if" makes us think about different possibilities for our life; it makes us imagine being in her situation. We are forced to consider how it might feel to live somewhere that you spoke a language you did not learn at birth.

Now the poet begins to develop an unpleasant extended metaphor. She imagines her tongue as a piece of meat in her mouth. She says that if you lived in a language you were not born into "your mother tongue would rot". The metaphor of rotting meat is distasteful. It is made worse by realising that the meat which is rotting is in her mouth and is her own tongue. The horror of this is underlined by her repetition of the word "rot" in line thirteen. She then says that the mother tongue or native language would "die in your mouth". The thought of something dead and decaying in your mouth is revolting. The poet is using our disgust to communicate how strongly she feels.

In line fourteen, the poet explains that with a dead piece of meat in her mouth, she is left with no option but to "spit it out". This phrase is repeated in the next line to communicate that this is a terrible thing. By living in a different language, the poet's own mother tongue has died and she has had to reject it. She has very effectively made us feel how awful this would be.

However, the direction of the poem now changes from horror to something mystical and lyrical. The poet says "but overnight while I dream". Here the poet reveals that even though she thinks the English language may have killed her Gujarati, it comes back in her dreams. The word "dream" has a double meaning here; it is both the moment of imagining when asleep and the idea of a wish or desire. Therefore the poem's deepest wish – to keep her mother tongue – comes true in her dreams.

Lines seventeen to thirty suddenly change where the reader thought the poem was heading. The lines alternate words in Gujarati and phonetically spelt words which express how to pronounce them out loud. The poet is doing two things here; first, she is showing us that her mother tongue is irrepressible, and secondly, she is inviting the reader, quite literally, to speak with her tongue in their mouth.

This is a celebratory moment – the poet's mother tongue has come back to her while she sleeps. She also wants to show the reader how much she loves Gujarati by getting us to join in with it. If the reader reads the phonetically spelt words in brackets underneath the Gujarati, then they can make the sounds of the language. We are thereby enabled to speak in a different language and to imagine what it feels like to be bi-lingual. It also makes us realise how lovely the sound of the poet's native language is; it makes us realise that we would not want to lose it either.

Having enjoyed the sound of the words, without knowing what they mean, the reader is given a translation of them into English. This begins on line thirty one. In stark contrast to the metaphor of the tongue as a piece of rotten meat, the lines describe the tongue as a lovely flower.

The poet writes, "it grows back". This is a joyful moment of resurrection. It is as though a miracle has happened and the dead tongue has returned to life. She describes the growth of the language as a "stump of a shoot". Therefore it begins tiny, but soon it "grows longer, grows moist, grows strong veins". The triple repetition of "grows" expresses the pace of the plant maturing. Each time the word "grows" is mentioned, the plant becomes healthier until it is full of blood and alive.

Instead of being a lump of rotting meat, the tongue is described in the extended metaphor as a "bud". A bud is the closed flower of a plant. It is usually a similar shape to a tongue, so this is a vivid image. The poet continues to describe how the "bud opens in my mouth, it pushes the other tongue aside". The mother tongue now re-establishes itself and finds a place inside her mouth.

The end of the poem sums up the poet's realisation that even though she thinks her mother tongue will die because she is immersed in the English language, it always returns to her – "Everytime I think I've forgotten". The final image is beautiful. The poet describes the bud opening in her mouth – "it blossoms". Blossom is the most lovely part of a tree; it opens in spring time, and usually represents new life, hopefulness and youth. Thus the poet leaves us with a positive image of a language and cultural identity inside herself which can never been destroyed.

POEMS WITH LOTS OF POTENTIAL COMPARISONS WITH THIS ONE

"Poem at Thirty Nine" – provides interesting juxtapositions between the ways the poets assert their identities, sometimes in a context which is unfriendly to them.

"Half caste" – provides excellent links to the poem because it is also about being proud of your identity.

"Remember" – provides useful comparisons because both poems are about a person trying to remember who they are.

POET

U.A. Fanthorpe (1929-2009)

Fanthorpe attended St Anne's College, Oxford where she received a First Class Degree in English before teaching at Cheltenham Ladies' College for sixteen years. She eventually turned her back on teaching to do a number of office jobs while writing poetry. She published her first volume of poetry, "Side Effects" in 1978 and went on to become the writer in residence at St Martin's College, Lancaster. In 1987 Fanthorpe started working full time as a writer, giving readings and producing a number of poetry collections. She died aged 79.

She was a Fellow of the Royal Society of Literature and received the Queen's Gold Medal for Poetry in 2003.

BACKGROUND

Fanthorpe's experiences as a teacher and Head of English permeate much of her poetry. This poem criticises the behaviour of teachers who fail to communicate clearly with their students. Ironically, the lesson the child is taught through the punishment is not the one the teacher intended. He learns about a world outside time, not that he should not behave in a certain way.

SUMMARY

The boy is being punished for a mistake which has not been adequately explained to him. The teacher gives the boy a detention, telling him to stay in the classroom until half-past two. However, because the boy has not yet been taught how to read the clock, he doesn't know when to leave. When the teacher forgets about the boy, he enters a world outside normal time, discovering an intense experience of the present which he remembers for the rest of his life.

ANALYSIS

The title of the poem, "Half-past Two", is the time which the child is told he must wait in the classroom until. It is the end of his detention. Ironically, in a poem with a named time in the title, the concept of doing things at specific times is overturned. Instead, the poem turns the title on its head as the times on the clock are dissolved and the boy learns about other forms of time, as well as how to enjoy the present.

The first stanza opens with an allusion to fairy tales – "Once upon a schooltime". The initial phrase is the conventional way that children's stories begin. It suggests that the poem will be occupied with a traditional fairy story; there will be a hero, a villain and an eventual happy ending. This is all true, but in this case it is the teacher who is the evil character. This challenges the reader's attitude to teachers and invites us to consider the lasting effects of their carelessness. The first line ends with the compound word "schooltime". This is not a real word; it is formed by putting two already existing words together to create a new one. This emphasizes the fact the story will take place during a special kind of time – the hours spent at school. The use of the compound word also makes the language sound childlike.

The entire poem is written using an unusual point of view - free indirect speech. This means the story is told in the third person using "he", but the words are those spoken or thought by the character who is being described. In this case, a boy too young to tell time. Free indirect speech is a technique often employed by writers when trying to express the inner emotions of a character who is not able to tell you them directly. This might be because the character is too young to be able to communicate fluently with the reader. Fanthorpe uses this technique effectively in the poem. A boy too young to read a clock is given a voice through the third person narrator in order to explain what it felt like to be abandoned and consequently outside time.

The use of childlike phrasing is continued in the next line "He did Something Very Wrong." The capital letters stress the words the child feels most deeply. They imply that he is echoing the words an adult has told him, but the way they are phrased suggests that he does not know what his crime is. The boy only knows he has done "Something" which his teacher deems "Very Wrong". The word "Wrong" could mean incorrect, but it also holds the implication of something morally frowned upon. The phrasing suggests the boy feels a terrible weight of adult disapproval, while not actually understanding what he did. The final line of the stanza is in parentheses or brackets – "(I forget what it was)". This dismissive phrase by the third person speaker shows that the child's wrong doing was clearly not very great as they cannot remember it. This is comic and ironic. There is a gap between the child's perception of events as very serious and the grown up speaker who realises that a small boy could not have done anything terribly bad.

The second stanza begins with a conjunction "And". Conjunctions are meant to connect two parts of a sentence together, but here it is used to open it. This shows the eagerness of the child's voice to explain what happened to him. The boy's anxiety is also expressed by his description of the teacher as "She" with a capital letter. This gives her almost godlike status. It underlines the importance of her words to him. Indeed the speaker repeats the phrase the boy has been told "Something Very Wrong". The repetition of the phrase and the capital letters emphasize the importance the event has for the boy, but the terrible irony is that he is being punished for a crime which has not been explained to him. Consequently, the learning experience has been entirely derailed. A punishment without a clear reason is simply cruel. The teacher has put him in detention and he must "Stay in the school-room till half-past two". Even worse, the teacher has not given the boy anything productive to do during the punishment; he must sit and wait. She is using boredom to reprimand the child, but the teacher's plan backfires as the boy is far from bored.

The third stanza is written entirely in parentheses. These brackets are used in writing to show an afterthought or piece of less important information. Here they highlight the way the teacher treats the child as an afterthought, something to be "forgotten". Fanthorpe is criticising the teacher's attitude to the boy. First, the teacher "Being cross" had "forgotten She hadn't taught him Time". Anger should not drive a teacher's treatment of a student. Secondly, the teacher has not taught the boy a crucial skill – to read the time. This makes her punishment impossible to implement. The stanza ends with the sad realisation that the boy is "too scared at being wicked to remind her". Therefore the boy's experience of education is clouded by fear; he is not able to speak to his teacher and consequently it is impossible for him to learn. The use of the word "wicked" here is telling. It suggests the sorts of words the teacher has used to tell the child off. It shows that he has been severely reprimanded and told he is evil or "wicked". This is out of step with the punishment the child receives and with the fact the teacher forgets completely about the boy and his crime by the end of the poem. Again, it shows that the teacher is misusing her power over the boy.

Stanzas four and five move on to the boy's experience of time. It explains that the child knows a variety of different types of time. The compound words used to describe the varieties of time - "Gettinguptime, timeyouwereofftime, Timetogohometime, TVtime" – show that from a child's point of view time is not the numbers on the clock, but the experiences which occur. The boy organises his day by the things he does. This seems a much more active way of seeing time as it is always an event. By contrast, the teacher has made time into something which does not have an event or activity – a perpetual waiting which is punishment. Stanza five ends by underlining that it is not that the child does not understand time: he does. It is just that his understanding of time is not bound to the clock, "All the important times he knew, But not half-past two". Fanthorpe is suggesting that the boy's experience of time is more real and "important" than the one that grownups use to rush through their day. As the poem is written in free verse with no set rhythm or rhyme scheme, the fact these two lines rhyme with each other "knew" and "two" makes them stand out all the more. Indeed they chime in the middle of the poem, summing up that the boy's understanding of time is more harmonious or pleasant sounding than our own.

In stanza six the narrator explains what the boy knows about telling the time. The description is an extended personification. The clock is compared to a person; it has "little eyes And two long legs for walking". This shows the childlike and innocent nature of the boy who sees the clock in a friendly way. However, the poem explains that although the boy knows what the marks on the clock look like "he couldn't click its language". It is interesting that Fanthorpe changes the conventional description of a clock's sound from tick to "click". This underlines the idea that the boy views clocks with a fresh new perspective. However, "click" sounds more mechanical and frightening than tick. It shows that the boy imagines the clock's noise to be a language he has not yet been taught, and because that language is clicking it seems to be inhuman and difficult. Again, the inadequacy of the boy's teacher is underlined here; surely she should have taught him how to read the clock.

Stanza seven begins with the word "So". This is synonymous with therefore. It shows the reader that the consequence of the boy not understanding clocks is that the following things happen to him. His waiting takes his mind "beyond onceupona". This implies that the boy's thoughts go past telling himself stories and imagining things. Instead the boy "knew he'd escaped for ever". The verb to escape suggests that the boy has been imprisoned. In a way he has been held captive in detention, but the boy has also been imprisoned in a larger sense – through the adult obsession with time keeping. The boy has managed to escape the idea of specific times when things must be done to find a world full of the present. It is ironic that his escape is described as "for ever" as there is no time where he has gone. There is only now.

The next stanza tries to depict what being absolutely present in a world without time might feel like. Every line of the stanza begins with the word "Into" to show that the boy is truly entering the world for the first time. Each line contains a sense – smell, hearing and touch – to show that the boy finds a world where how things feel is everything. He joins "the smell of old chrysanthemums on Her desk" and "the silent noise his hangnail made". There is an oxymoron in the phrase "silent noise". This means that even though the two words contradict each other, when put together they show us a startling experience. Here the boy is able to hear the sound of his own snagged nail because everything else in the world is so quiet. The boy's growing self-awareness ultimately enables him to enter "the air outside the window, into ever". Thus he is able to leave normal reality and become a part of the natural world.

However, just as the boy reaches a state of absolute contentment with the world around him, the teacher finds him. The teacher is described "Scuttling in". This metaphor imagines the teacher as a beetle or insect moving in a scampering way. It underlines her lack of human feeling towards the child. She reveals "I forgot all about you". Thus the boy is not important to her; she is a poor teacher. She sends him home, "Run along or you'll be late". Immediately the boy is put back into an adult timetable where there is rushing and the possibility of lateness. Stanza ten goes on to describe how she "slotted him back into schooltime". The teacher has destroyed the boy's positive experience of the world and returned him to a realm of deferral, where he must wait for "teatime, Nexttime, notimeforthatnowtime".

The final stanza leaves the reader with some hope. The boy "never forgot how once by not knowing time, He escaped into the clockless land". Therefore the child did learn something from school. Ironically, it was not the lesson his teacher meant to teach him. The boy learnt through experience a world beyond adult time. The poem ends with an extended metaphor describing the "clockless land". This returns the poem to the diction of the fairy tale where there are exciting new kingdoms. In this land the poem personifies time hiding. It is as though time does not want to be found and exploited by human beings. Time is "tick-less waiting to be born". Therefore time is an unborn foetus not yet brought into existence. The ticking would mark its life in the world. Cleverly, time is left waiting in this land in the same way the boy was left waiting in the classroom. The poem concludes with the idea that waiting and being inactive could actually be an exciting and illuminating experience.

POEMS WITH LOTS OF POTENTIAL COMPARISONS WITH THIS ONE

"Prayer Before Birth" – provides strong links with the poem. Like Fanthorpe's boy, the unborn child recognises some of the evils of the world.

"Piano" – provides comparisons with the themes of memory and time.

"Hide and Seek" – provides many comparisons between the experiences of being forgotten or abandoned as a child and what this teaches.

6. "Piano" by D. H. Lawrence

POET

David Herbert Richards Lawrence (1885-1930)

D.H. Lawrence is a famous English novelist, who also wrote essays and poetry. He was born into a mining family in Nottinghamshire. His working-class background influenced his belief in the dehumanising effects of industrialisation. He won a scholarship to attend Nottingham High School and then trained as a teacher. He fell in love with the wife of his university lecturer, and they ran away together to Europe. Lawrence spent much of his life travelling and working around the globe. However, Lawrence was eventually diagnosed with tuberculosis and this meant he had to settle in the warm climate of northern Italy and travel less. It was here he wrote his most famous novel, "Lady Chatterley's Lover" (1928) which was notorious for its explicit sex scenes.

BACKGROUND

Lawrence's mother, Lydia, was a remarkable woman. Before marrying, she had worked as a pupil teacher; she valued the importance of education to liberate the working classes from the drudgery of factory life. However, her husband's financial problems meant she had to take manual work in a lace factory in order to support their family. She made sacrifices for her children, and harboured great ambitions for her clever son. She encouraged Lawrence in his academic and artistic endeavours and was a formative influence on his opinions, and ultimate success.

SUMMARY

The poem describes an involuntarily triggered memory of the poet's mother. As he listens to a woman singing, he is reminded of his mother singing to him as he sat underneath her piano. The poet tries to remain in the present, but the memory is too strong, and he is ultimately pulled back into the past. He is left crying for his lost childhood and dead mother.

ANALYSIS

The title of the poem "Piano" describes the instrument Lawrence's mother used to play to him. It is the focus of the memory he is about to describe. A piano is also a musical instrument which expresses emotion. This is like the poet, whose memory of his mother produces an emotional response in him which is expressed in the form of poetry rather than music. Finally, "piano" is also a direction in music; it is an Italian word. It means a piece of music should be played softly. This suggests the poem describes a soft and heartfelt moment.

Indeed the first word of the poem is "Softly", echoing the musical meaning of the title. The word presumably also describes what the music sounds like that Lawrence is listening to. "in the dusk" or the early evening of the day, the poet hears a woman "singing to me". The fact the poem takes place at "dusk" provides an atmosphere of sadness. This is the time of day when the light is fading and the night time is approaching. Metaphorically, it seems the poet is about to face a dark moment in his life. Moreover, "dusk" is also the hinge of the day, connecting day and night. In the poem, the poet occupies a pivotal position between the past and present of his life. Therefore the time the singing takes place is very important.

The woman who sings in the present is not described in detail. However, her singing is "to me". So it is personal and directed at the poet. This moment of a woman expressing her feelings to the poet through music is juxtaposed with the memory he is about to have of his mother expressing her love for him through her own singing. Here sound becomes a trigger for memory. The poet can do nothing to prevent the memory of his mother flooding back. In line two the trigger occurs – "Taking me back down the vista of years". His memory is described in visual terms; a vista is a pleasing view. Thus Lawrence is carried to a picture in the far distance of his life "till I see". The verb to see here is a powerful one. It shows how vivid the memory is. The poet is not imagining the past, he has actually returned to it and is watching it in front of him.

Line three begins with "A child sitting under the piano". It is fascinating that the child is described using the indefinite article or "a". The poet does not make clear this is a specific child. At this point, the memory is obviously personal, but the language is keeping it universal for us all to imagine ourselves in. This also underlines the fact, the poet is standing back and watching his own memory. The child is "sitting under the piano". This description places the child in an intimate position with the instrument and the woman. It is as though he is nestled somewhere safe. The memory seems to focus here on his mother as a place of shelter. In another way, the position of the boy also shows the dominance of his mother. She is high above him creating the music, while he is a fledgling artist, listening and learning.

The description goes on to depict the boy "in the boom of the tingling strings". Because the child is under the piano, he is in the heart of the vibrating instrument. The onomatopoeia of "boom" communicates vividly to the reader the sound of the piano. Clearly, from his position beneath the instrument, the boy hears the music very loudly. This is a contrast to the singing of the woman at the start of the poem. It suggests that the past is somehow more real, more loud than the present. The strings of the piano are described as "tingling". This is a personification. If something tingles, then it moves, creating a feeling of excitement. The piano is portraying the pitch of excitement the boy beneath it feels.

The final line of the stanza focuses even more deeply on why this moment is so exciting. The boy is "pressing the small, poised feet of a mother who smiles as she sings". Therefore the boy is touching his mother's feet while she sings. Notice again, that the mother is described with the indefinite article "a", like the child in line three. This makes the personal nature of the act more universal. It also suggests that the poet is standing back and watching his younger self and his mother from a distance. This distance is produced by time passing, but it is also a way for him to observe himself and possibly restrain his emotional response to the memory.

The mother's feet are "poised" because pianos require their players to press pedals with their feet to either sustain, dampen or shorten the notes. Her feet are controlling the length of the notes; this might relate to how sustained and prolonged the memory is. Moreover, the boy is "pressing" the feet. That means, he is involved in her playing in a very intimate way. Not only is the boy touching his mother affectionately, showing a loving connection, he is also learning from her feet by mimicking and following them with his hands. The mother "smiles as she sings". This description shows that she enjoys the intimacy this act affords them. It is a moment of shared pleasure and learning for both boy and mother.

Stanza two brings the reader back to the specific emotions of the poet – "In spite of myself". This means the poet wants to resist the memory. However, he describes "the insidious mastery of song". The word "insidious" means something cunning and underhand. This means the woman singing has gained "mastery" or power over him in a sneaky and sinister way. The poet goes on to say, the music "Betrays me back". This is an odd phrase which would not be used in conversation. When someone is betrayed, information about them is disclosed to an enemy. Here the singing of the woman in the present has treacherously exposed the poet to his own past. This underlines the fact he does not want to return to the past, even though it appears to be a happy place.

The poet explains that the memory pulls him "back" until "the heart of me weeps". This is a powerful metaphor. It is not just that he cries; it is his heart – the location of love – which cries. His heart is weeping because it wants to "belong To the old Sunday evenings at home". Thus the core of himself, his heart, wants to return home, while his head is resisting because it knows the past can never truly be visited. He goes on to describe those evenings "with winter outside, And hymns in the cozy parlor". The fact it is winter, gives the interior scene a sense of comfort and shelter from the cold. The poet's mother was clearly playing hymns on the piano because it was Sunday, a day of religious worship. The stanza ends with "the tinkling piano our guide." Here the piano is described as "tinkling". This onomatopoeia is very different from the "boom" employed earlier. This is a pleasing, soft, sound. It is the poet's "guide". That means, the piano music leads or guides him back to his past.

Stanza three begins with the word "So". This is synonymous with therefore. The poet has been fighting his emotions for two stanzas, but now we are to be told the consequence of this. The next word "now" returns the reader to the present emotion of the poet. We have left the cosy parlour. In this moment in the present, the poet explains "it is vain for the singer to burst into clamor With the great black piano appassionato". The word "vain" means pointless. The poet is saying there is no point in the singer of the present erupting into "clamor" or a loud noise with the piano playing "appassionato". This is another Italian term used to instruct how to play an instrument. In this case it means to perform with a great amount of emotion.

The reason there is no point in the singer bursting into a loud, emotional crescendo is because the poet has already been transported to an intense moment of feeling through the memory. He explains "The glamour Of childish days is upon me". The word "glamour" means something appealing or magical. Therefore the poet's memories of childhood have enchanted him. He continues, "my manhood is cast Down in the flood of remembrance." This describes the way the memory has taken away his manliness or stoicism. "cast down" means thrown aside. Thus the poet has discarded any pretence of appearing brave. This is due to the "flood of remembrance". This metaphor compares the way the memory has overcome him, with a tidal wave of water. It shows how powerful and overwhelming this has been.

The poem ends with the sentence, "I weep like a child for the past". This is a simile. The poet is crying in the way a child would cry. That suggests, he is uncontrollable in his tears. Importantly, his weeping is "for the past". So, the poet is crying because he longs for the past to be alive again. Thus the poem charts the poet's initial resistance to a memory which deeply saddens him. Eventually, he is defeated by its power, and cries for his lost past.

POEMS WITH LOTS OF POTENTIAL COMPARISONS WITH THIS ONE

"Half-past Two" – provides useful comparisons as both poems are about an adult remembering a childhood event which was formative.

"Do not go gentle into that good night" – provides powerful connections as both poems are about the love the poet holds for a parent who is dead or dying.

"Remember" – provides interesting points of comparison with this poem as they are both about memories after the death of a loved one.

7. "Hide and Seek" by Vernon Scannell

POET

Vernon Scannell (1922-2007)

Scannell was born in Lincolnshire to a poor family who moved around the country a lot to find work. He left school at fourteen to take a job in an insurance office. In 1940 he enlisted in the army. He fought in the North African desert. However, he was court-martialled for desertion after walking away from his fellow soldiers when they looted and abused the dead after a key battle. He was sentenced to three years' imprisonment in a military prison; he served six months and was released to fight in the Normandy landings. Following the end of the war in Europe, he deserted again and spent two years on the run. He was eventually arrested in 1947 and sent to a military hospital. On his release, Scannell went to London where he supported himself through teaching and boxing professionally. This gave him time to write poetry.

He published many poems in his lifetime and became a Fellow of the Royal Society of Literature.

BACKGROUND

Scannell writes a number of poems about the pains of childhood. Many of them are focussed specifically on his son. His time in the army made him particularly sensitive to injustice and cruelty. This is evident in the poem.

SUMMARY

The poem describes a children's game of hide and seek. The boy thinks he is clever to hide in the shed. The searchers laugh outside the door, but do not find him. After a very long time, the boy emerges, thinking he is the winner, only to discover his friends have abandoned him as part of a cruel trick.

ANALYSIS

Like much of Scannell's work, the title of the poem, "Hide and Seek", has an obvious and a deeper meaning. The obvious meaning is that the poem will describe the children's game of hide and seek. The deeper meaning is about the game as a metaphor for growing up. It suggests that all people experience a process of discovery about the world which often reveals the cruelties of others.

The poem is written in one long stanza. This gives it a sense of concentration and focus. The reader must pay attention to the details of the game which become increasingly significant. The poem is told from the point of view of a third person poetic voice which speaks to the child and also describes how he feels. The first line of the poem is an instruction from the poetic voice "Call out. Call loud". This is a double imperative from the narrator to the character in the poem. This could sound dictatorial, but the voice advises the boy wisely throughout the poem. Thus the voice becomes a helpful friend to the child. This highlights the fact which emerges fully at the end of the poem, that the child does not have any other friends. The voice could also be interpreted as expressing the inner thoughts of the boy; it is as though he is encouraging and instructing himself.

The first line gives us the voice of the child "'I'm ready! Come and find me!'". This piece of dialogue at the beginning of the poem provides a sense of the boy's character. He seems excited, friendly and happy. It is a stark contrast to the tone at the end of the poem. It also makes the poem seem quite dramatic and immediate; the reader is involved in a scene which is about to unfold. The drama of the poem is enhanced by using the present tense. The entire poem is written as though it is happening while we read it. This is an effective technique which transports the reader to the moment of the game, and places us within the action as it happens.

Next we discover where the boy is hiding, "The sacks in the toolshed smell like the seaside". The simile here is effective because it reminds us of playful times at the beach. This suggests that the boy is happy in his hiding place. The poetic voice goes on to reassure him, "They'll never find you in this salty dark". The metaphor here is an interesting one. "salty dark" mixes two different senses: taste and sight. This makes the image powerful, showing that the boy's senses are more alert than normal because he has no light in the shed. The poetic voice continues to advise the boy on how to hide without being found –"be careful that your feet aren't sticking out. Wiser not to risk another shout". These pieces of advice add to the feeling of excitement and enjoyment in the opening of the poem.

The next section of the poem from line six to ten describes the discomfort of hiding and the boy's attempts to hear what the searchers are doing. In line six the floor is "cold". This is the first hint that something more sinister might be happening. The poetic voice describes the boy's thought process. He is wondering what the other children are doing – "They'll probably be searching The bushes near the swing". The importance of the game is underlined by the narrator who advises the boy that "Whatever happens" he should not sneeze. This sense of there being a lot at stake in the game increases the excitement the reader feels. The narrator goes on to imagine the behaviour of the seekers when they find the boy as "prowling in". This is an image with lots of implications. The verb personifies the searchers as animals. "prowling" means to move stealthily, usually in pursuit of prey. Therefore the children have started to be described as predators hunting for their victim. This escalates the impending danger in the poem, placing the hiding boy in the role of victim.

Line nine begins a new sentence with a conjunction, "And". These are meant to connect two parts of a sentence, not to introduce one. By using it at the beginning of the sentence, the poet is showing the abrupt surprise the boy feels when he realises the searchers are outside the door – "And here they are, whispering". The fact the other children are "whispering" is made more suspicious by the next line which tells us, "You've never heard them sound so hushed before". The idea of "whispering" suggests that there is a secret being discussed. It excludes the boy from the activity of the seekers and makes the reader feel concerned.

In line eleven the poetic voice tells the boy "Don't breathe. Don't move. Stay dumb." This triplet of three imperatives instructs the hiding child how to behave if he wants to evade detection. Each of the orders builds on the tension of the scene as we see how hard the child is trying not to be found, how much effort he is prepared to give to win the game. However, the final instruction "Stay dumb" has more sinister connotations. "dumb" means to remain silent, but it also suggests the more colloquial meaning of remaining stupid or ignorant. It seems the poetic voice may be noticing that the boy is foolishly not understanding the trick his friends are about to play on him or it might be wishing that he could remain innocent or ignorant of cruel pranks forever. Either way, the word seems even more worrying when we reach the next sentence – "Hide in your blindness." This metaphor describes the boy in the darkness of the shed. However, it imagines him as blind, unable to see at all. This implies that he is blind to what is actually happening to him. He doesn't realise he is the victim of a prank.

Outside the shed, the boy hears the other children "moving closer". The poetic voice then says "Their words and laughter scuffle". This is a metaphor. It gives the voices of the searchers a human movement – a "scuffle". This usually means a small fight. Therefore the boys who are looking for the child are being described in aggressive terms. The boy is advised in line fourteen "don't come out just yet". He thinks he is winning because they have not searched the shed. The poem goes on to say "They must think that you're very clever". Here we see the pride of the hiding child as he begins to believe he has defeated all the others in the game. If the reader has read the poem carefully, then they will be feeling increasingly anxious for the boy as his perception of events is not accurate. He views the behaviour of his friends with innocence, whereas the experienced and older reader can see that things are not as they seem.

By line eighteen even the boy is realising that the game has lasted longer than usual – "It seems a long time since they went away". At this point the description of the boy's location begins to become more sinister. His legs are "stiff" and "the cold bites through your coat". The personification of the cold trying to take chunks out of his body with its teeth is disturbing. The description continues with the deadening sound of the alliteration on the letter 'd' in "dark damp smell". This time, the smell "moves in your throat". Coupled with the biting, the idea of a smell which occupies the boy's throat depicts him as being assaulted by nature. It is as though the garden has turned on him, trying to wound and suffocate him.

The poetic voice now advises the boy "It's time to let them know that you're the winner". Up until this point, the poem has been structured with rhyming couplets every five lines. For example, "out" and "shout", "door" and "before", "lane" and "again", and finally, "coat" and "throat". These infrequent rhymes give the poem a sense of harmony and happiness. However, from the moment the boy decides to emerge from the shed, the rhymes disappear. This implies that the jolly and childlike world which he used to occupy is ending.

The boy emerges from the shed calling, "I've won" Here I am". His triumph is in stark contrast with the final lines of the poem – "The darkening garden watches". This personification of the garden describes it as getting darker or more sinister, and observing the behaviour of the boy. The fact the garden stands back and watches, but does not help the boy makes him seem even more isolated and friendless. The next short sentence tell us "Nothing stirs". The sense of emptiness is emphasized here. The boy is alone in the garden and the other children have deserted the game.

In line twenty four "The bushes hold their breath". This personification describes the bushes like a person waiting for something to happen. Someone holds their breath because they are expecting an event; in this case the event is the realisation that the boy has been abandoned. The poet now uses pathetic fallacy or the technique of using the environment, and especially the weather, to mirror a character's feeling – "the sun is gone". This not only tells us that it is the end of the day and the game has lasted a long time, it also communicates a powerful image of the loss of light and goodness from the boy's world.

The final line of the poem is a rhetorical question; a type of sentence designed to influence the reader by asking them to think about a particular idea. The poetic voice says to the boy, "Yes, here you are. But where are they who sought you?" The question is left hanging at the end of the poem, meaning the story never gets resolved. There is no happy ending. Moreover, the question makes the reader think about where the other boys have gone. Like the boy, the reader now discovers the truth; his friends have deserted him. The wider implication of this story is that growing up involves realising that people will not always support you, and that the world will not necessarily be your friend.

POEMS WITH LOTS OF POTENTIAL COMPARISONS WITH THIS ONE

"Prayer Before Birth" – provides interesting contrasts between an unborn child who already knows that human beings are cruel and the child in the poem who has to learn this.

"Blessing" – provides comparisons between children enjoying themselves together in adversity and the children in this poem who turn their game into an act of bullying.

"Half-past Two" – provides a strong comparison between a child who is let down by grown ups only to learn a positive lesson about life, and the boy in this poem who is disappointed by other children and learns a harsh lesson about life.

8. Sonnet 116 by William Shakespeare

POET

William Shakespeare (1564-1616)

Shakespeare was an English poet, playwright, and actor. He is most famous for his 37 plays. He was brought up in Stratford-upon-Avon where he married Anne Hathaway at the age of 18. They had three children: Susanna, and twins Hamnet and Judith. Between 1585 and 1592, Shakespeare moved to London, becoming a successful actor, writer and owner of a theatre company. He returned to Stratford-upon-Avon an enormous success in 1613. He died three years later, aged 52.

BACKGROUND

Sonnets are fourteen line poems with a set rhythm and rhyme scheme. They were invented in the mediaeval period in Italy. The rhythm is iambic pentameter which means there are ten syllables in every line and every second syllable is always stressed or emphasized. The rhyme scheme of a sonnet depends on whether it is an Italian/Petrarchan sonnet or an English/Shakespearean sonnet. Here the rhyme scheme is the one made famous by Shakespeare and which was later given his name: ABAB CDCD EFEF GG. This means the sonnet is divided into three sets of four lines which rhyme together, called quatrains. At the end of the sonnet, the two lines are meant to rhyme with each other as a sort of conclusion or summary – these lines are called a rhyming couplet. Sonnets were the novels of their day; they were written in sequences with each sonnet forming another chapter in a story. That is why this sonnet is number 116. Shakespeare actually wrote 154 sonnets in his collection. Sonnets were traditionally written by aristocratic men with titles to show off their cleverness. By contrast, Shakespeare came from a relatively poor background; his father was a glove maker. The traditional subject of sonnets is the adoration of a female Beloved figure who is beautiful, but too pure and religious to consider human love. By contrast, Shakespeare wrote 126 of his sonnets to a young male friend, and only 28 sonnets to a Dark Lady with whom the poetic voice has a passionate sexual relationship. Many critics view the poems as autobiographical, but there is little evidence for this. More likely, Shakespeare took all the traditional ingredients of a sonnet sequence and turned them on their heads to show how original and clever he was. Shakespeare's sonnets may be an attempt by him to be seen as a more serious and inventive writer. It may seem surprising to us, but in Shakespeare's life time the writing of plays was considered great entertainment, but not necessarily great art.

SUMMARY

The sonnet attempts to explain and define what true love is. The requirements of perfect love become increasingly difficult to express and to achieve during the course of the poem. The end of the sonnet leaves the reader wondering if a true love is something we can ever attain in the real world.

ANALYSIS

The first line of the sonnet plunges the reader into the middle of a thought. The poet says that he does not want to allow "impediments" or obstacles to "the marriage of true minds". The word "impediments" alludes to the marriage service which pauses to ask if any of the congregation know of any obstacles to the couple's marriage. Thus immediately the poem places us in the world of married love. However, the phrase "marriage of true minds" is interesting. Here the poet seems to be saying that only people who bring together "true minds" should be allowed to marry. This is locating the site of love in the mind or head. It is not about hearts being brought together, or even bodies. Instead, Shakespeare is suggesting that the only sort of love which should be allowed to exist is one which is based on spiritual or intellectual compatibility. This immediately sets the bar very high and begins a discussion about what true love really is.

This attempt to define or explain true love is clearly a painful one for the poet as the sonnet is peppered with nine negative words – "not", "no" and "never" – repeated again and again. It is as though Shakespeare finds perfect love so difficult to explain that he can only describe it by saying what it is not. For instance, in line two the poet says "love is not love". He goes on to explain that real love does not alter "when it alteration finds, or bends with the remover to remove". This is suggesting that one of the key aspects of true love is constancy. It does not change. However, Shakespeare's description is stronger than this. He is saying that a lover should not stop loving, not only if their Beloved changes, but also if their Beloved removes their love. He is suggesting true love will not be flexible or "bend" with the Beloved if they decide to "remove" that love. In one way, this sounds faithful and true, but in another, this could be seen as frighteningly single minded, and lacking in an appreciation of the partner's wishes to leave the relationship.

Indeed, the complexity of this idea of never changing is expressed at the start of line five, when the poet exclaims "O". This is an outburst of emotion. It appears Shakespeare is really pushing himself to make sense of the concept of love. He goes on, "O no, it is an ever-fixed mark". This is another image of constancy. This metaphor compares love to a "mark" which cannot move. The steadiness of love seems very positive here. However, the word "mark" does not only mean a point, it sometimes means a stain. This could be describing love as a stain which cannot be washed out. It is a mark which brands you forever. Again, this is highlighting the fact that a perfect love may be something so difficult to achieve that it is not even possible in the real world.

In line six, Shakespeare introduces the metaphor of a storm. He explains true love "looks on tempests and is never shaken". A tempest is a tumultuous storm. Therefore love is not altered by the troubled moments in a relationship. He offers us another metaphor; this time love is "the star to every wandering bark". A "bark" is a ship. Here the ship is "wandering". The verb makes the boat sound aimless or lost. The metaphor compares love with a star which would have been used by sailors to navigate ships in the past. Therefore love is a guide in life which helps you when you are off course. This is a lovely image. The metaphor is extended on line eight; here the poet describes the star as an entity "Whose worth's unknown, although his height be taken". In order to navigate by the stars, sailors would use a sextant to calculate the angle from the pole star. This would allow them to work out what direction to go in. Shakespeare's detailed description shows that while some aspects of the star can be measured or "taken", the vast majority of its wonder remains "unknown". If the star is like love, then this suggests that love will forever be something we cannot fully know or appreciate wholly.

Shakespeare changes direction here to introduce a new image of love. This metaphor is also a personification. The poet says "Love's not Time's fool". Here Shakespeare is saying real love will not perform like a jester in the court of Time's kingdom. In other words, real love is not made fun of by the years passing. Shakespeare explains this in more detail by imagining the beauties of youth, the "rosy lips and cheeks" which Time will destroy with his "bending sickle". This is an image of time as the Grim Reaper, a figure with a blade to cut down human life. Therefore true love will not diminish even when the Beloved is no longer beautiful and young.

Again, the poet repeats that real love will not change in line eleven. He says it "alters not with his brief hours and weeks". Instead, love "bears it out even to the edge of doom". The word "doom" here alludes to Doomsday or Judgement Day in the Bible. It was believed that the world would end on Doomsday when God would return to the earth and judge all the souls, both living and dead once and for all. After this time, the world would be destroyed. Therefore Shakespeare is saying that true love "bears it out". The verb to bear suggests carrying a burden or doing something strenuous and difficult. Thus a perfect love must remain faithful to their Beloved not only during life, but also after it. They must remain in love in the afterlife, until God returns to decide their fate or judge them. This sort of love, beyond our own death and the death of our loved one, is almost unimaginable, and yet Shakespeare is saying that our love is not true unless we can do this.

By this stage of the sonnet, the reader is coming to realise that Shakespeare has set the bar so high for love that it almost seems impossible to reach. We have to wonder if any couple could really live up to such high standards of fidelity and constancy.

In lines thirteen and fourteen, Shakespeare moves to the rhyming couplet. In traditional sonnets, this should be a happy summary of the poem's content. However, this seems to be impossible for Shakespeare to do, having spent twelve lines of verse tying himself and the reader up in knots about the lofty standards of true love. Indeed the first word of the couplet suggests that a conclusion is not going to be easy because it begins with "If". This word is a conditional. It says that something is only true when other conditions or circumstances are met. The poet says "If this be error". This makes him sound uncertain as to whether or not he has adequately described true love. It seems to wonder if he has made a mistake or an "error". However, the last line claims that if he is wrong about love then "I never writ". This is one thing we can be sure of, Shakespeare clearly did write. Apart from all the plays, he has also just written the first 115 sonnets of his sequence. Therefore this suggests that it must be true; this must really be what love is. Yet the line goes on to say "nor no man ever loved". This means there are three negatives in one line "never", "nor" and "no". All these negatives do ultimately suggest that what Shakespeare is describing must be correct or no man has "ever loved", but they mount up making the reader feel uncertain.

The uncertainty is only added to by the rhyme in the rhyming couplet. The last two lines of an English or Shakespearean sonnet are meant to rhyme with each other to provide a happy conclusion, but here "proved" and "loved" appear to rhyme on paper, but when read aloud do not. They are what is called a half rhyme. Thus Shakespeare has ended his poem defining the beauty of love with a deformed and misshapen couplet. It is as though the whole idea of people coming together in a perfect union is deconstructed in this rhyme; if a couplet explaining love cannot reach harmony and perfection, then how can a couple of human beings hope to live up to Shakespeare's standards of love.

The sonnet leaves us wondering if true love can ever be described, and if true love can ever be achieved.

POEMS WITH LOTS OF POTENTIAL COMPARISONS WITH THIS ONE

"La Belle Dame Sans Merci" – provides interesting comparisons with this sonnet as it describes an unhealthy type of love in which the man is emasculated by the Beloved.

"My Last Duchess" – provides a contrasting view of love. Unlike Shakespeare's sonnet, the poem describes a love that changes with sinister consequences.

"Remember" – provides strong comparisons as it is also a sonnet about love which challenges the traditional subject matter and poetic voice of the form.

9. "La Belle Dame Sans Merci" by John Keats

POET

John Keats (1795-1821)

John Keats was part of the Romantic movement in poetry. This was a reaction to the Industrial Revolution and the Enlightenment which sought to find beauty and wisdom in nature and emotion.

Keats was born to a lower middle class family; his father ran an Inn in London. He was sent to a school in Enfield where he developed a love of classics and history. When Keats was 8 his father died, and when he was 14 his mother died. In the same year as his mother's death, Keats was sent to become an apprentice to a doctor.

In 1815 he began studying medicine at Guy's Hospital. However, Keats just wanted to write poetry. Having qualified as a doctor, he encountered ill health and began to devote all his time to writing, relying on his siblings for money. In 1818 Keats fell in love with Fanny Brawne, an Inn keeper's daughter. At this time, he was also caring for his younger brother, Tom who was suffering from tuberculosis. Because Keats could not make enough money from his poetry, he was unable to marry Brawne.

In 1820 Keats fell gravely ill with tuberculosis. He was told to go to a warmer climate to help his lungs; he left for Rome, knowing he would probably not live to see Brawne again. He died in Rome five months later in 1821. When the news reached Brawne, she was distraught and stayed in mourning for 6 years.

BACKGROUND

The poem was written in 1819 when Keats was deeply in love with Brawne, but knew that he would never be financially-successful enough to marry her.

SUMMARY

The poem is a conversation. A speaker finds a knight weak and ill on a hillside. The speaker asks what is wrong with the Knight, and he explains that he met a beautiful woman who bewitched him. The woman took him to her magical cave where she put him to sleep. While asleep, the Knight dreamt of all the noble men enslaved and destroyed by love of a beautiful woman. When he woke, he found himself left on the hillside alone.

ANALYSIS

The title of the poem, "La Belle Dame sans Merci" is French. It means - the beautiful lady without pity. This immediately tells the reader that the poem will involve a cruel woman who has no sympathy for others. The title is borrowed from a 15th century French poem by Alain Chartier. The original is written in Old French. This allusion sets the scene of the poem which takes place in medieval times where there are knights and fairies.

The poem is written in the ballad form. This was a medieval structure for poetry which was designed to be performed to listeners. It makes the poem like a sad song. The poem is divided into ballad stanzas. These are four line verses, or quatrains, with an iambic, or unstressed followed by a stressed syllable, rhythm. Interestingly, Keats makes the fourth line of each stanza end on an unstressed rather than a stressed. This means every stanza ends on a dull note which makes the poem feel unresolved and sad.

The first stanza begins with an emotional exclamation – "O". This shows us that there is something wrong which is alarming to the speaker of the poem. The poetic voice goes on to ask a question, "what can ail thee". The word "ail" is a deliberately old fashioned one. Here Keats has selected archaic diction to create the impression that the story takes place in the medieval period. The question means what is making you sick. Therefore we know that someone is unwell at the start of the poem.

The character who is suffering is now introduced. He is a "knight-at-arms". These knights were warriors of the medieval period who bore arms or swords and were usually involved in a noble mission to help someone vulnerable. However, here the knight is "Alone and palely loitering". This means he is without company. Importantly, this suggests he is without his horse. This makes him symbolically unmanned. He has lost a vital part of his power. He looks sick as he is "palely loitering". The word "loitering" means waiting without a purpose. This is something a knight should never do; he should always be involved in a mission to help others. These details show us something dreadful must have happened to the knight.

The speaker describes where they have found the knight – "The sedge has withered from the lake, And no birds sing". The landscape depicted here is not just wintery – it is unnatural. Sedge is a plant which grows in boggy areas. However, it has died and the birds seem to have left the lake. This pathetic fallacy, or use of the setting to mirror the mood of the character, suggests that the knight has found himself in an unnatural and deadly environment.

The question the speaker asks in the first stanza is repeated in the second, but with varied words which emphasize the knight's poor condition. The speaker asks again "what can ail thee", but this time the knight is "haggard" or drained with suffering, and he is "woe-begone" or miserable in appearance. This reinforces the reader's assumption that the knight has endured a horror.

The speaker continues to describe the season. It is winter because the squirrel has collected food, so his "granary is full" and the "harvest's done". The crops are harvested in autumn. The speaker then describes the knight's appearance in more detail in stanza three. The knight has "a lily on thy brow". This metaphor suggests the man's forehead is as white as the flower, a lily. Lilies were associated with death, but they were also a symbol of the Virgin Mary. Therefore the image effeminizes the knight, making him seem womanly. His face is covered in sweat due to "anguish". This means severe mental distress, and he seems to have a "fever". The knight's complexion is losing its pink colour as "a fading rose fast withereth too" on his cheek. This is another metaphor from the world of flowers. Roses are often used to symbolise love, but here the rose is dying, so the knight's love must be abandoning him. Ironically, in a poem about a beautiful woman without pity, the speaker is kind, concerned and sympathetic. This becomes a stark contrast to the being who has bewitched, enslaved and abandoned the knight.

The rest of the poem is the knight's answer to the speaker; his explanation of what has happened to him. In stanza five he says "I met a lady in the meads". However, the woman he found in the meadows was not a human. Although she was "Full beautiful" or physically gorgeous, she was "a faery's child". This means she was a supernatural being or fairy. He describes her attractions. She has long hair, a "light" or graceful step, and "her eyes were wild". This final detail is alarming. If the fairy's eyes are "wild" then she may be full of malice. She is a supernatural force.

The knight is immediately in love with her. We can tell this because he stops whatever mission he is on and devotes his time instead to making love tokens for her. He says he "made a garland for her head". This means he plaited together flowers to make a crown for her. He also makes "bracelets" from flowers. This is a feminine thing to do, and something which draws the knight away from the human world and into the realm of the natural. He even creates a "fragrant zone" for her. This is a belt of flowers to go round her waist. In response to his gestures, the fairy looks at him "as she did love". The key word is "as" here. It tells us that she just appears to love him; it is not real. The "sweet moan" that she makes suggests that the knight and fairy become sexually intimate.

Symbolically, the knight gives the fairy his manly power. This is shown when he puts her on "my pacing steed". A steed is a horse. By setting the fairy on his stallion, the knight has raised her above himself, given her the masculine power of a horse, and placed himself in the position of a servant or squire, walking beside her. He is obsessed and enslaved by her. This is underlined in the next line which explains "And nothing else saw all day long". She fills his world by leaning over him and singing "A Faery's song". The song could be a spell, bewitching the knight.

The fairy then takes control of the knight fully. She feeds him natural food. She gives him "roots of relish sweet and honey wild, and manna dew". The first two of these items are found in nature, but "manna" is a magical and holy food which is meant to come from heaven. The fairy speaks to him in a "language strange". This shows us that she is not part of the knight's normal world. She is clearly alien and foreign to him, yet he still understands her. This might suggest that the words of women are strange to men; that the genders speak in different languages when it comes to love. The fairy tells him "I love thee true". This is the only time we hear the fairy's voice; her speech is quoted by the knight. Because we are never able to hear what she thinks directly, the poem gives us a very one-sided, masculine view of love.

The fairy takes the knight to her "elfin grot". Elves are types of supernatural beings, like fairies. They are meant to live in caves or grottoes. Thus she takes the knight home and there "she wept and sighed full sore". The fairy's tears and exclamations may be parts of her terrible seduction. They might also imply that the knight does not really understand her true nature. Indeed, in response to her weeping he shuts her "wild wild eyes with kisses four". The repetition of the world "wild" suggests that he finds her so feral and intimidating that he has to close her eyes, so he does not have to look into them anymore.

In the cave, the fairy "lulled" the knight to sleep. It is as though she is taking him even more deeply away from the real world and plunging him into a frightening realm of love which takes away his manly power. Asleep, he dreams. The knight exclaims "Ah! woe betide!" This is an outpouring of emotion. The expression "woe betide" means sadness happened. The grief the knight feels arises from having to recollect the dream he had.

Stanzas ten and eleven describe the dream. He "saw pale kings and princes too, pale warriors". Therefore his dream is filled with noble, powerful men who have become pale or sickly. The reason for their illness is explained because they "cried" to him, "La Belle Dame sans Merci Thee hath in thrall." The fact they cry suggests they are distressed. It is startling and worrying to see such powerful figures in such a terrible state. Their explanation for their downfall is that the beautiful lady without pity has turned them into her slaves. This is the crux of the poem. It is a symbolic description of the way beautiful women can make otherwise powerful men their playthings through the devotion of love.

The knight looks at the consequences of love for these men. They have "starved lips" in the gloom" or gloomy light. This implies they have been left unnourished by the fairy. She has made them fall in love with her, only to abandon them to starvation. Their mouths "gaped wide" in "horrid warning". The men are communicating with the knight and warning him not to let the fairy enslave him. The knight explains he woke from this dream to find himself "on the cold hill's side". He has returned to the conscious world, but without his lover he feels that winter has come and he has no purpose.

The final stanza sums up his situation. The knight explains "this is why I sojourn here". A sojourn is a temporary stay. The knight can no longer find a permanent home because the fairy has taken him away from normal life. The end of the poem echoes the lines spoken by the anonymous speaker in the first stanza, but they answer the question. The story we have heard is why the knight is on his own and "loitering" even though the "sedge is withered" and "no birds sing". Therefore we receive an answer, but it is not a resolution.

The poem ends with the knight unable to move on. He cannot seem to leave the hillside. He is stuck in a moment of obsessive love which he cannot escape. The fairy has made him a slave to love.

POEMS WITH LOTS OF POTENTIAL COMPARISONS WITH THIS ONE

"Piano" – provides comparisons with this poem because they are both about the power of a much-loved woman to control a man.

"Sonnet 116" – provides useful comparisons with this poem because they both offer different descriptions of what love is.

"The Tyger" – provides useful comparisons with this poem as they both depict a powerful and beautiful force which is beyond nature and our control.

"My Last Duchess" – provides useful comparisons because it offers a different view of gender relationships in which the man is the powerful one.

10. "Poem at Thirty-Nine" by Alice Walker

POET

Alice Maisenior Walker (1944-Present)

Alice Walker is an American novelist, poet and political activist. She wrote "The Color Purple" in 1982, winning the National Book Award for it and the Pulitzer Prize for Fiction. She was born in Georgia to a poor family; her mother worked as a maid and her father worked on a farm. Her mother believed in the importance of education to liberate her children, and Alice won a scholarship to university, graduating from Sarah Lawrence College. After university, she became interested in the Civil Rights movement in the 1960s and campaigned for equal voting, welfare and education rights in Mississippi.

She married Melvyn Leventhal, a Jewish civil rights lawyer; when they moved to Mississippi in 1967 they became the first legally married inter-racial couple in the state. They were threatened by the Ku Klux Klan and experienced great prejudice, but they remained in the state working to gain rights for other black and Jewish people.

BACKGROUND

Walker's father died in 1974. He did not live to see her success in 1982 with "The Color Purple", which was a best-selling and critically-acclaimed novel. The book describes the difficult lives of black women in 1930s Georgia where they are oppressed not only by the white laws and attitudes, but also by the black patriarchy. The poem was written in 1983 after Walker faced some harsh criticism of her novel for exposing negative aspects of black male culture.

SUMMARY

The poem describes how much Walker misses her dead father. She explains all the wonderful things he taught her about life, and concludes that although he may not have agreed with all her opinions, she believes he would be proud of her at this point in her life – at thirty-nine years old.

ANALYSIS

The title of the poem is very precise. It tells the reader that this was written when the poet was thirty nine. It implies that there was some sort of epiphany or realisation at this age, which is after the success of her novel, "The Color Purple". Interestingly, this age is often associated with the end of youth and the beginning of middle age. Perhaps it implies that this is a pivotal moment for Walker when she is finally able to reconcile with her father's memory.

The poem is written in free verse with no fixed rhythm or rhyme scheme. Nevertheless, the short lines create a staccato effect, suggesting to the reader that the poet is both emotional and determined to deal with a difficult subject in a precise way. The poem is also structured around a refrain – "How I miss my father". This is repeated twice in the poem. The second time it is mentioned, it has an exclamation mark, suggesting the poet is becoming increasingly emotional and upset as the poem progresses.

The first line of the poem is "How I miss my father." It is one short sentence which sums up the content and tone of the rest of the poem. It is almost exclamatory, an outpouring of the emotion of bereavement and loss. The expression is quite colloquial, giving the poem a chatty feeling, which enables the reader to relate profoundly to the voice of the poet; it is as though she is confiding in us about her grief. The word "How" implies that missing her father is a great and multifaceted emotion. The possessive pronoun "my" adds to the sense that this is very personal; it is about the poet's own father, no one else's. This is a deeply personal expression of grief.

The first stanza goes on to say "I wish he had not been so tired when I was born". The verb to wish here gives the impression that there are things the poet wants to change about the past; she has a desire or dream she wants to happen. This suggests that there may be regrets about her relationship with her father. The description she then gives of her father is one of exhaustion; he was "so tired". This directs the reader to the biographical details of Walker's life; her father was a poor farmer who worked very hard to make ends meet. Walker is explaining to herself and her father that his exhaustion due to hard work took him away from her. Indeed from the moment she was "born" her father was perhaps too tired to engage with her in the way she wanted.

The next stanza moves on to the reason for her father's tiredness. It is dominated by descriptions of money. The poet explains that she is prompted to "think of" her father when she is "Writing deposit slips and checks". This is how money is entered into a bank account and withdrawn from it to pay bills. It seems surprising to the reader, that it is this moment of business-like activity which reminds the poet of her father; it doesn't seem very intimate. This underlines the impression that the poet's father was preoccupied with work and financial troubles during his life. The poet explains "He taught me how". Her father taught her how to write the bank forms, "This is the form, he must have said". It is interesting that the poet's memory of her father has to be reconstructed, "he must have said". This does not sound as though the poet remembers the details of the lesson; she has to make assumptions about how he taught her. This underlines for the reader how personal the memory is, and how we all have very different memories of events which are often changed over time.

The poet goes on to explain that her father's emphasis on money taught her to see "bits of paper as a way to escape the life he knew". This is ironic. It is her father's lesson about his own life with money which makes the poet want not to be like him. The verb to escape is important here. The life her father led and which her family therefore experienced was clearly a difficult one. The necessity of escape suggests their life was like a prison, that they were held captive by poverty. Thus money is the way to find freedom. The poet notes that "even in high school" she had a "savings account". High school is the American equivalent of the GCSE and A level years in Britain from, the age of fourteen to eighteen. The poet is quite unusual therefore in already saving money during her teen age years and making financial plans for the future to avoid her father's fate. Furthermore, the poet uses the idea of "bits of paper" to confuse the reader. As she is a famous novelist, the reader probably thinks these "bits of paper" are the beginnings of her writing, and that these would enable her "to escape" poverty. However, we then realise that the papers Walker refers to are indicative of her desire to achieve financial security and not her dream of becoming a writer.

The third stanza gives us another lesson Walker's father taught her – "He taught me that telling the truth did not always mean a beating". This is another double-edged description. At first sight, it suggests that Walker's father was a fair and lenient man. It implies that if Walker was honest about a mistake then her father would not harshly punish her. The word "beating" is shocking to us, but in the past children were hit by their parents for misdemeanours. Nevertheless, "beating" implies an extremely violent response. Walker may be hinting here at the subject of her novel, the violent and abusive lives of poor black Americans. The notion of being beaten for being honest may also have a political implication. Black Americans were unfairly, and sometimes violently, treated by the police and authorities for simply going about their business. Walker may be suggesting that her father taught her to be honest despite the cruelty of the society in which she lived. This would then be a lesson in political defiance.

Walker goes on to end the third stanza with a touching thought. She explains that "many of my truths must have grieved him before the end". Here Walker is coming to terms with the fact that the honest expression of her beliefs during her life probably caused her father great sorrow; the word "grieved" usually means to feel bereavement for a loved one. Here the bereavement seems to be metaphorical. Walker imagines her father feeling a sense of bereavement at the way she lived her life. Perhaps her father felt that he had actually lost her to a lifestyle he could not comprehend or approve of. Again, this is ironic. Her father taught her to be fearlessly honest, but this honesty was a source of unhappiness for him. Walker chose a difficult life of political protest as part of a mixed race couple. This would have been shocking to many Americans, and possibly to her father. It is also the case that Walker's novel, "The Color Purple" describes violent and abusive black men. These characters were seen by some critics as a terrible affront to the black community, suggesting that black people might be as cruel to each other as white people are to them. Thus Walker is coming to terms with the fact her father taught her well, but the way she expressed his teachings might have hurt him, and for this she is sorry.

This is a moment of intense personal honesty and emotion. It is understandable therefore that the next stanza begins with the repetition of the opening line of the poem, this time with an exclamation mark – "How I miss my father!" Walker seems overwhelmed with grief. She possibly wants the opportunity to speak to her dead father and explain her actions; find a reconciliation with him. Obviously, this is not possible after someone has died. Instead, Walker takes the only route she knows to reach her father – she writes this poem about him.

Walker goes on to enjoy a memory of another lesson her father taught her – "He cooked like a person dancing". This simile is joyful. It describes Walker's father doing a task which many might consider a chore or perhaps something better suited to a woman. Yet Walker's father cooks with the pleasure and physical abandon of someone dancing. She elaborates the image. While moving, her father concentrates "in a yoga meditation". Yoga is a Hindu spiritual discipline which involves certain physical postures as well as controlled breathing, and an attempt to clear the mind of busy thoughts. Thus Walker's father cooks with concentration and an almost religious calm. She goes on to explain why cooking is so important to him. He "craved the voluptuous sharing of good food". The word "craved" is significant here. If something is "craved" then it is desired almost to the point of addiction. Therefore her father passionately wanted to share food with others. The act of sharing suggests he was a friendly and sociable man, who loved his friends and family. The word "voluptuous" means opulent and pleasure loving. This is in stark contrast to the description of him in the second stanza when he is worried about money.

The penultimate stanza begins with the word "Now". It brings the reader back to the present day from remembering the past. It tells us the influence her father has had on Walker – "I look and cook just like him". She sees her dead father most in herself when she is cooking because her "brain" is "light". This image suggests cooking provides a moment when her mind is not heavy with thoughts. The description of cooking now becomes a metaphor. The way Walker cooks is compared to the way she lives, "seasoning none of my life the same way twice". This suggests that like a good cook who adds appropriate quantities of salt and pepper according to the taste of a dish each time it is made, Walker lives her life in a constantly adapting and thrilling way. The metaphor of "seasoning" a dish also implies that Walker always spices up her life and lives in an exciting and responsive way. The stanza concludes with "happy to feed whoever strays my way". The verb to stray suggests someone homeless who wanders in. Thus Walker, extends her father's friendliness, to include any strangers who want to join her table. She is welcoming of others.

The final stanza shows that Walker has moved beyond the terrible feeling of loss and bereavement with which the poem began, and has convinced herself that although she has lived her life differently from her father, she is still like him. She writes "He would have grown to admire the woman I've become". Here she acknowledges that her father might not have immediately liked all her actions, but that he would have "grown" or found a way to appreciate her. The final description is about Walker, not her father. She sums herself up as someone who is "cooking, writing, chopping wood, staring into the fire". These activities begin with cooking and writing which we already know about. However, "chopping wood" shows us that she is also physically strong and able to do stereotypically-male tasks. Finally the image of her "staring into the fire" shows that she is a woman who can provide for herself both physically and spiritually; she chops the wood for her own fire, and she is able to stare at it in contemplation because she is also a woman of great ideas.

Therefore the poem begins full of sadness and loss, but ends with a realisation of the poet's own worth which she believes her father would have appreciated.

POEMS WITH LOTS OF POTENTIAL COMPARISONS WITH THIS ONE

"If" – provides useful comparisons as it is the reverse of Walker's verse – it is a poem in which a father gives advice to a child.

"Search for my Tongue" – provides useful comparisons as both poems are about how identity is formed by our earliest experiences.

"Piano" – provides useful comparisons. Both poems are concerned with remembering a dead parent.

"Do not go gentle into that good night" - provides useful comparisons as it is also about the conflicting emotions felt at the loss of a parent.

"Remember" – provides useful comparisons as it is also about how to remember loved ones who have died.

11. "War Photographer" by Carol Ann Duffy

POET

Carol Ann Duffy (1955-Present)

Carol Ann Duffy is Britain's Poet Laureate. She is the first woman to be appointed to this position. She was born to a working class Catholic family in Glasgow. Her family moved to Stafford when she was six. She always wanted to be a writer, and she began publishing her poetry when she was only 15. When she was 16, Duffy entered into a relationship with a famous Liverpool poet, Adrian Henri. She went to Liverpool University to be with him, where she studied Philosophy.

She has worked as a poetry critic, and a lecturer in poetry. She has published many collections of poems and won a number of awards. Her work is often distinguished by the way it gives a voice to the voiceless of society.

BACKGROUND

The poem was inspired by a real life friendship with a war photographer; a professional cameraman sent into areas of conflict around the world to capture the news in pictures. In conversation with him, Duffy realised the issues involved in communicating horrible events.

SUMMARY

The poem describes a war photographer who has returned to England. While developing the horrific photographs of war-torn locations around the world, the photographer contemplates the indifference of the people who look at his work in Sunday newspapers.

ANALYSIS

The title tells us immediately that this is about the profession of the man, and not an intimate portrait of someone; the experience of the "War Photographer" is depicted as something universal which we can learn from. The poem is structured around four stanzas of six lines. The final two lines of each stanza are a rhyming couplet. The rigid rhyme and rhythm of the poem might appear surprising when it is concerned with something so emotional, but the point Duffy is making is portrayed effectively by this calm. Duffy is communicating the apathy of the newspaper readers, so to have a structure which does not startle is appropriate.

The first stanza dramatically places the photographer at work. He is "In his darkroom". Interestingly, the poem describes the photographer in a place of safety and familiarity. He is not out in a war zone working. Indeed, the next phrase suggests this calm place of darkness is a sanctuary for him – "he is finally alone". The word "finally" implies that the man has been surrounded by people and noisy situations from which he is grateful to retreat. The next line employs clever sibilance; he has "spools of suffering set out". A spool is a cylinder on which the film of a camera is wound. To develop the film, it has to be removed from the spool and dipped in chemicals. The reels of film are full of "suffering" or pain, but they are "set out in ordered rows". This suggests that the photographer may observe the pain of war, but he is not part of it. He is able ultimately to organise it in a calm and controlled way.

The only light allowed in a darkroom is "red and softly glows". This is a necessity as other types of light deteriorate film, but here Duffy makes the red light symbolic. Red is a colour often associated with danger. It is a warning sign. However, she is showing the reader that all the danger has been transformed into something which "softly glows". It has been made gentle and appealing. The photographer has taken the horror of a real situation and turned it into a picture which can be viewed from a position of safety and comfort. She goes on to introduce a simile, "as thought this were a church and he a priest". The darkroom is compared to a Catholic church in this image. In Catholic churches a red light burns continuously to symbolise the presence of the blood of Christ. Thus the photographer is like a priest communicating Christ's suffering to his congregation. This places the photographer in a religious and evangelising role. He is meant to bring the suffering of the world to our attention.

Duffy explains he is about to "intone a Mass". Mass is a religious service which remembers Christ's sacrifice by giving worshippers bread and wine. The bread and wine represent Christ's body and blood which were tortured and killed at the crucifixion. Therefore the photographer developing his pictures is like a priest reminding his congregation of a terrible death which happened to save their souls. The stanza ends with the names of three famous war zones: "Belfast. Beirut. Phnom Penh." Each city is given a separate sentence to show its importance. Belfast was the site of fierce Irish Republican conflict since 1970. Beirut is a city in Lebanon where a terrible civil war from 1975 to 1990 cost a quarter of a million citizens their lives. Phnom Penh is the capital of Cambodia which was taken over by the ruthless Khmer Rouge and their leader Pol Pot. Between 1975 and 1979, he orchestrated the systematic killing of two million Cambodians who disagreed with his communist regime. Duffy is employing the allusive nature of these names to make the reader think about the horrors which have occurred in the world and which have been photographed.

The final phrase of the first stanza is a quote from the Bible – "All flesh is grass". This famous phrase comes from the Old Testament Book of Isiah. The metaphor means that human beings are like grass; we are fragile and easily cut down. The expression explains that we will all die. Coming after the names of places where killings have occurred, it serves as a timely reminder that just because we live in the apparent safety of a rich and privileged country, like Great Britain, death and suffering can reach us too.

The second stanza focuses on the importance of the photographer's work – "He has a job to do". His job is both developing the film in the darkroom, and risking his life to take the pictures. Sibilance is used again in "Solutions slop in trays". These are not only the chemicals used to develop the pictures spilling, but also the idea of solutions or answers to questions which are contained "beneath his hands". The photographer is shaking as he watches the horrible images appear as the film is placed in the chemicals. Duffy notes that he did "not tremble" when he took the pictures, but now that he is safe he is able to take in the horror and allow his emotions out.

The stanza moves on to explaining the photographer's home. He is in "Rural England". Rural means the countryside. The phrase conjures up idyllic images of cottages and fields of corn. This is done to juxtapose the places the photographer has travelled to, which are destroyed by violence. Duffy explains that "Home" is a place of "ordinary pain which simple weather can dispel". She is suggesting that the pain which occurs in England is not comparable to that experienced in war zones and that a spell of sunshine can "dispel" or get rid of it. She repeats this idea, describing the fields "which don't explode", highlighting how safe our world is. Unlike the field where "running children" are killed in "a nightmare heat". This seems to be another historical allusion. One of the most famous war photographs was taken by Nick Ut during the Vietnam War in 1972. The iconic photograph depicts a group of children running and crying on a path through a field after they have been burnt in a napalm attack. Duffy is reminding the reader of the difference between the lives of children in war zones and those lucky enough to live in rural England.

The third stanza describes the image of the photograph becoming visible in the chemical tray – "Something is happening". She then describes the picture. There is a stranger's face, "a half-formed ghost". The metaphor of the stranger being like a ghost, suggests that they may now be dead and that the picture has captured them and kept them present after death. The photographer "remembers the cries of this man's wife". The photograph seems to be of a man who is dying; his wife is weeping while he suffers. The photographer remembers how he "sought approval without words to do what someone must". Here the photographer is communicating with the dying man through looks because he cannot speak his language. He wants "approval". This means permission to photograph the man's dying moments. The photographer justifies this invasion of the man's and his family's privacy because "someone must". In other words, it is important that these events are recorded for the world to see in order to stop the suffering. The photographer is reminded of "how the blood stained into foreign dust". This is a description of the stranger bleeding into the earth. The fact it leaves a stain suggests that his death will have a lasting meaning because the photographer can show the world what happened in his picture.

However, this justification seems misplaced as the final stanza explains that people are not paying attention to his pictures. The photographs depict "A hundred agonies in black and white". Therefore the photographer takes many images of the pain of others, but his "editor will pick out five or six". Thus many of these powerful photographs will be discarded and unused. Only a few will be chosen to appear in "Sunday's supplement". This is a reference to the magazine or "supplement" which accompanies newspapers on a Sunday. They often run stories with lots of photographs about serious issues around the world.

Although the pictures are being printed and communicated to the world, they seem to have little effect on their viewers. Duffy says "The reader's eyeballs prick with tears between the bath and pre-lunch beers." This suggests that people read the magazine on a Sunday morning and feel briefly upset by them, but actually their enjoyable lives continue. They are exposed to the horrible images between having a relaxing bath and a drink before a roast. The routine of the lives of the readers implies that the pictures do not change them or make them want to change the world. Their "tears" are momentary.

The poem ends with the photographer setting off on another trip to a war zone. "From the aeroplane" he looks at England. He "stares impassively". This means he looks at his own country without emotion. It is as though he cannot understand why his fellow countrymen are not more moved by his work. Duffy concludes the readers "do not care". We are left with the suggestion that because we live such comfortable lives in England we do not have empathy for others; when we see suffering we cannot be bothered to help. It is a bleak ending.

POEMS WITH LOTS OF POTENTIAL COMPARISONS WITH THIS ONE

"Prayer Before Birth" – provides lots of comparisons with this poem as they are both about the cruelty of the world.

"Blessing" – provides a strong contrast with this poem as it depicts a moment of joy within a context of poverty and suffering.

"The Tyger" – provides interesting comparisons with this poem as they are both about the relentless nature of cruelty in the world.

12. "The Tyger" by William Blake

POET

William Blake (1757-1827)

William Blake is a famous English poet and artist. He was born into a working class London family and only attended school until he was ten years old. He was an early influence upon the Romantic Movement in art which tried to redress the dehumanising effects of the Industrial Revolution through a return to nature and the past. Blake was a radical and original thinker who admired the ambitions of the French and American Revolutions to bring equality to the masses. He was also a committed Christian whose non-conformist faith is evident in many of his works.

His most famous poems were published in 1794, called "Songs of Innocence and Experience". The book contained two collections of poems; one was called Innocence and the other Experience. The "Songs" juxtapose poems which contrast a childlike perception of the world, with poems about the loss of that innocent view.

BACKGROUND

"The Tyger" is located in the Experience section of the "Songs". It is therefore part of the grouping of poems told from the point of view of an experienced speaker who has lost a childlike view of the world. In the 1790s in London there were few opportunities to see tigers. Therefore the animals had a mythic status as powerful beasts. The spelling of tiger is odd in the poem because at the time Blake was writing the spellings of words had not yet been fixed.

SUMMARY

The poem is spoken directly to a tiger. The speaker asks the tiger what sort of a creator would make an animal which is both beautiful and deadly. The poem dwells on this thought, but never provides an adequate answer. Instead, it communicates the poet's wonder at the way God is responsible for bringing both goodness and evil to mankind.

ANALYSIS

The title of the poem describes its focus; it is not only about a tiger – it is spoken to a tiger. The first stanza of the poem addresses the animal in one long sentence. The rhythm and rhyme scheme of the poem have a clear structure. Each line of the poem has seven syllables. The seven syllables are divided into trochees or a stressed syllable followed by an unstressed syllable. This means the lines have a strong rhythm, like the beating of a hammer or the padding of stealthy paws. Because the last syllable of every line ends with an unstressed, there is a sense of something left unfinished. This reflects the way the poem fails to answer the speaker's question, communicating instead how difficult it is to understand God. The rhyme scheme of the poem is AABB. This uniformity again provides a strong impression of the pounding of the tiger's feet.

The poem opens with a call to the beast "Tyger, Tyger". There is alliteration not only of the 't' sound which creates a staccato, stealthy opening, but also of the following 'b' sound in "burning bright". This is a metaphor describing the tiger actually alight or in flame. This description captures the mottled orange colour of the tiger vividly. However, it also highlights the dangerous and beautiful nature of the animal. Like fire, the tiger is deadly, but also magical.

The stanza concludes with a question – "What immortal hand or eye, Could frame thy fearful symmetry?" This is the question which dominates the entire poem; it asks what "immortal", or what type of god, would "frame", or create, the tiger's "fearful symmetry", or terrifying symmetrically-patterned being. Here the tiger does not simply represent an apex predator, it also symbolises the idea of destruction in the world. Blake's question may seem silly at first sight, but if it is considered in greater depth, we see that it gets to the heart of man's experience of the world. Blake is asking a question all of us must have wondered about at one time or another – if God is good then why has he created a world with both kindness and cruelty in it.

The reader will notice that the first and final stanzas are essentially the same. They are both the same question addressed to the tiger, wondering what sort of god would have brought destruction to the world. However, there is one word which is different from stanza one. In the first stanza the poet wonders who "could" or is able to "frame" the tiger, while in the final stanza, Blake asks who would "Dare frame" it. The word "dare" here means be brave or bold enough to create it. Thus the thoughts of the speaker of the poem have progressed from wondering who would create evil to wondering who would be reckless enough to create it. Therefore the speaker's anxiety is not alleviated in the poem. By the end of the poem, they feel even more horrified by the fact God deliberately created evil to prey on mankind.

The second stanza wonders where the tiger must have been created. It is important to notice here that every sentence in the poem is a question apart from one in line sixteen. This repeated question structure suggests the way the speaker cannot get beyond the thought of God making evil; his question just keeps cycling through the poem, never finding an answer.

The poet describes the "distant deeps or skies" where the creator must have found "fire" for the tiger's "eyes". This description underlines the extremity of the beast, as a creator must have gone to the very top and bottom of the universe to search out the correct element to make the animal. The poet goes on to wonder "On what wings dare he aspire?" This uses the metaphor of flying to suggest the lofty ambition God must have had when he made the tiger. The last line of the stanza imagines God's hand which must "seize the fire" to create the animal. This image is relatable to the reader; we can imagine the bravery and foolhardiness needed to take fire in one's hands. This suggests that the tiger is made from materials such as flame which are more commonly associated with hell rather than heaven. This begins the suggestion that God may not be as meek and mild as Christians think.

Stanza three develops this thought. It begins with a conjunction "And". Conjunctions are meant to connect two parts of a sentence. Here it introduces one, showing that the speaker is in a rush of ideas, desperately trying to express his fear and wonder. The poet goes on to wonder at the effort which must have been necessary to make the tiger, "what shoulder, & what art, could twist the sinews of thy heart?" Strangely, the creator is imagined here with powerful shoulders used to bend and form the muscles of the tiger's heart. Again, Blake is challenging the reader to see God in a more powerful and frightening way. This idea of the power of the creator is underlined in the last line of the stanza which wonders at "What dread hand? & what dread feet?" Here the poet cleverly challenges the reader. The "dread" or terrifying "hand" could be God's, while the "dread feet" could belong to either the animal or the creator. Blake is bringing the tiger and God together here to show that someone who makes such a ferocious beast, might also be ferocious themselves.

The next stanza develops this unusual view of God. Here God is described through an extended metaphor as a blacksmith working at a furnace. This could also be a description of the newly-built factories of the Industrial Revolution where men worked long hours in terrible conditions, often smelting metal in massive fires. The poet wonders at what sort of "hammer", "chain" and "furnace" were required to make the "brain" of the tiger. This focus on the mind of the tiger as made of metal and formed in fire is terrifying. It suggests the beast has great strength, endurance and power. The description goes on to imagine the "anvil" where the tiger's brain must have been beaten into shape. An anvil is a heavy iron block on which metal is hammered out. This metaphor not only depicts an awe-inspiring beast, it also creates a frightening view of God.

God in this stanza is a burly blacksmith whose muscles are used to twist and shape the ferocious tiger. This is startling. God is being described here through imagery we normally associate with hell and the Devil; he is a God of fire, muscle and "dread". The shocking nature of this description is emphasized in the punctuation. The verse ends with an exclamation mark, "Dare its deadly terrors clasp!" The exclamation mark suggests the poet is overwhelmed by the thought of a muscular God creating the tiger in a fire.

The penultimate stanza imagines what happened after the tiger was created and unleashed on the world, "the stars threw down their spears And water'd heaven with their tears". The stars are personified here. Stars are often associated with heaven. It is possible the stars represent the disapproval of the heavens at God's creation of the tiger. The stars throw down "spears". This might mean that the stars are trying to hunt down the tiger and kill it before it does any damage. However, the description could also mean that the stars "threw down" or discarded their spears in a protest against violence when they were confronted by the tiger. Whichever reading you choose, the stars are ultimately dismayed by the creation of the animal; they weep. This sense of heavenly sorrow is scary; even the universe thinks the tiger is a bad idea.

This stanza ends with two questions: "Did he smile his work to see?" Here "he" is God. The poet is wondering could God really be pleased with himself when he realised what he had created. He concludes "Did he who made the Lamb make thee?" The lamb is an important symbol here. Most obviously, a lamb is a gentle, vegetarian animal which is normally the food for vicious animals like the tiger. Therefore the poet is asking how could God create both the hunter, or tiger, and the hunted, or lamb. In other words, why would God create an entire system on earth based upon the conflict between powerful animals and their victims.

This image of the lamb has even deeper meanings. The lamb is a religious symbol of Christ. This is because lambs are innocents who are killed; this is like Jesus who was pure and good, but was executed by mankind. Thus the allusion to the lamb also suggests that the poet is wondering why God made both Jesus and the Devil; why God made both goodness and evil, both victim and villain, both hunted and hunter, both bullied and bully. He is making the reader think about the opportunity God must have had to create a world without cruelty and death. Instead, he chose to create the tiger.

Therefore the poem ends with the same question with which it began, suggesting there has not been an answer found which adequately explains God's actions in making the tiger.

Moreover, the replacement of the word "could" with "Dare" leaves the reader dwelling upon the reckless nature of a god who created the ultimate killing machine to prey upon mankind.

POEMS WITH LOTS OF POTENTIAL COMPARISONS WITH THIS ONE

"Prayer Before Birth" – provides useful comparisons as both poetic voices are trapped by their wonder at the cruelties of the world.

"War Photographer" – provides points of comparison as both poems show a speaker who wants the world to notice the horror which exists.

POET

Robert Browning (1812-1889)

Browning is an English poet who is famous for writing poems in the dramatic monologue form.

He was born in Surrey. His father was a well-paid administrator at the Bank of England and his grandfather was a wealthy slave owner in the West Indies. His father was an avid collector of books who encouraged his children to pursue the arts. His mother was a devout non-conformist. By the age of 12, Browning had written his first collection of poems. He studied Greek at University College, London. He devoted his life to writing poetry, remaining at home with his parents until he was 34, when he married the poet Elizabeth Barrett. Her father disapproved of her marrying anyone, and so the couple moved to Italy where they had a son and lived out the rest of their lives.

BACKGROUND

The poem is based on real characters from history. The speaker is Duke Alfonso II who ruled northern Italy, Ferrara, from 1559-97. His title was the Duke of Ferrara. His first wife was Lucrezia de Medici. She was fifteen years old when she married him, and she died two years later in 1561. There were suspicions that she had been poisoned. The poem is set in 1564, three years after her death. A negotiator has arrived from the Count of Tyrol to arrange for the Duke to marry his daughter. The Duke married three times during his life time. The artist who painted Lucrezia's picture is also an historical figure, Fra Pandolf, who was a celebrated portrait painter.

SUMMARY

The poem is spoken by the character of the Duke of Ferrara. He is showing a man who has arrived to organise his marriage to a new woman, a portrait of his dead first wife. While the Duke describes his first wife, the reader begins to suspect that something dreadful may have happened to her.

ANALYSIS

The poem is written in the form of a dramatic monologue. A monologue is a speech given by one character. Here the character is the Duke of Ferrara. We do not hear any other voices. The poem is entirely his voice telling a gentleman about his wife. The reason the monologue is called dramatic is because it is like a scene from a play or film. It captures a dramatic moment which takes place in a specific time and place which we are allowed to watch, like an audience in a theatre. The Duke is speaking to an ambassador or negotiator who has come to arrange his marriage to the daughter of his boss. The entire poem takes place with the Duke standing in front of a portrait of his first wife, describing it to the ambassador. The dramatic monologue form is used to create convincing characters in poetry. These characters then reveal their identities through what they say. The form encourages the reader to read between the lines of what the character says to find the truth.

The poem is one long verse. This can make it difficult to read, but if you break it into sentences, it becomes easier. It is written in iambic pentameter with every two lines rhyming

– rhyming couplets. There is lots of enjambment, or poetry lines which run the sentences on. This is all done to give the effect of real speech patterns.

The title of the poem "My Last Duchess" is significant. It tells us the speaker is using a possessive pronoun "My" to show he owns the woman. The word "Last" informs us that she is his previous wife. It suggests that there will be more wives. This immediately hints to the reader that the speaker is quite callous about his relationships with women. The subheading "Ferrara" tells us the poem takes place in northern Italy and makes clear that this is based on the historical character of Duke Alfonso II.

The first line throws us into the middle of a conversation. The Duke is pointing out a picture of his first wife, "That's my last Duchess". The picture is a painting which captures the woman "Looking as if she were alive". The phrase "as if" tells us that the woman is no longer alive; she is dead. Instead of speaking sadly about his deceased wife, the Duke goes on to describe the painter who made the picture. He says the artist was "Fra Pandolf". Immediately, we see the Duke likes to boast that he has great pieces of art made by famous artists. The Duke invites the ambassador to "sit and look at her". This places the negotiator in the position of the reader, patiently watching the Duke explain the picture to us.

The Duke explains that "none puts by The curtain I have drawn for you, but I". This tells us that the picture is concealed behind a curtain which the Duke has opened for the ambassador to view the painting. The curtain is symbolic here. It tells the reader that the Duke does not like sharing his possessions with others. He covers up a picture so only he can see it. It also suggests he enjoys being in control. Only he can open the curtain, therefore he likes having power over others. This begins to ring alarm bells for the reader. The Duke is not making a good impression; he sounds controlling and selfish.

The Duke reveals that the face in the picture has an "earnest glance". The word "earnest" means both serious and sincere. Browning wants the reader to picture the scene and imagine the painting itself. We imagine the face of a young girl with a serious expression. The word "glance" not only describes someone's look, it also suggests that she only looks up briefly. Again, this is creating a picture of the Duchess as a lovely, diffident and serious girl. The Duke goes on to say that "Strangers", like the ambassador, always ask "How such a glance came there" when they see the portrait. Therefore the Duchess's anxious look has prompted others to ask what caused her to look so serious. This makes the reader wonder how her husband treated the Duchess to make her look so solemn at such a young age.

The Duke says that the Duchess was not made happy only by her "husband's presence". This is an odd thing to say. Only a very controlling person, would expect their wife to be made happy only when they are around. It tells us that the Duke expected his wife only to enjoy his company and have no other pleasures. This implies that the Duke treated his Duchess as an object that he owned and controlled.

The Duke goes on to give examples of some things which made the Duchess look pleased. He says "perhaps" compliments from the painter called up that "spot of joy". The word "perhaps" implies that the Duke actually does not have any facts about this matter; he is speculating because this is what he believes. This strikes the reader as paranoid and unfair. The phrase "spot of joy" is an interesting one. The metaphor describes a look of pleasure as a "spot". A spot is something small, but it is also something which marks or taints. It is something which should not naturally be there. This tells us that the Duke does not like his wife looking or being happy. This does not bode well for their marriage. The implication here is that the Duke believes his wife has committed adultery.

The Duke explains his wife had a heart "too soon made glad, Too easily impressed". Both these emotions are positive, but the word "too" which introduces them shows that the Duke thinks his wife is excessively happy and admiring of others. He is turning her good qualities against her. He continues to describe her character as someone who "liked whate'er She looked on". This implies she was a happy and positive person who always saw the best in things. However, the Duke says "her looks went everywhere". He is implying that he wanted to control what she was able to see. The theme of sight recurs throughout the poem. This is unsurprising in a piece about looking at a picture, but the theme is developed in interesting ways. There are lots of instances of perception and misperception to show that things might not be the way they initially appear. This is to encourage the reader to look below the surface and judge the Duke's behaviour.

The Duke explains "'twas all one". This means that everything his wife saw was treated with equal respect and appreciation. Again, this would be a positive quality for most people, but for the Duke it is a sign that she is unable to appreciate his superiority. He continues with examples of the things his wife enjoyed such as "The dropping of the daylight in the West, The bough of cherries" and the "white mule she rode". These are all natural things which she takes pleasure in. She loves the sunset, delicious fruit, and pretty animals. Clearly, the Duchess does not value expensive things; she likes the ordinary pleasures of the world. The fact this annoys her husband suggests that he is much more materialistic and elitist. He only wants her to like things which involve him and which are considered valuable by others.

The Duke explains "She thanked men…as if she ranked My gift of a nine-hundred-years-old name With anybody's gift". This highlights the way the Duke believes his wife should be grateful to him for marrying her, for giving her his name. The idea of a wife being given her husband's name upon marriage as a valuable gift is telling. The changing of a woman's name underlines that she has been taken into the possession or property of her husband. The Duke thinks his wife should appreciate his name as not only a sign she belongs to him, but also a privilege because it is an ancient title which has been passed down for almost a millennium. The Duke thinks she only values his status as much as her mule and he dislikes this.

The Duke's rhetorical question highlights how much he is irritated by his wife's lack of materialism. He asks "Who'd stoop to blame This sort of trifling?" The word "trifling" means treating him as though he is unimportant. The Duke thinks his wife does not show him enough respect. He wonders what sort of person would "stoop" or diminish themselves "to blame" or to tell off someone for this behaviour. Therefore the Duke is too proud to lower himself to his wife's level and tell her he does not like her happy attitude to life.

The character of the Duke is further revealed when he digresses. He says "Even had you skill In speech – (which I have not)". The phrase in brackets or parentheses, shows that he claims not to be able to speak well, but this is clearly not true. He has just bent the ambassador's ear without pausing; the Duke clearly likes the sound of his own voice very much.

The Duke says that he thought about telling his wife "'Just this or that in you disgusts me; here you miss or there exceed the mark'". This rehearsal of lines he thought about delivering to his wife discloses the personality of the Duke who uses very strong language to describe his wife's attitude. If you find something disgusting then it is repulsive, and if you do not meet the mark then you fail to live up to a pre-set standard. The Duke clearly judges his wife very harshly as though she were a servant rather than a partner.

However, the Duke explains that he does not want to teach his wife or help her to "be lessoned". He believes "E'en then would be some stooping; and I choose Never to stoop." The Duke repeats the word "stoop" to emphasize his belief that speaking to his wife would involve him losing his superior status or bowing down to her, and he is not prepared to do this.

The Duke explains that as his wife smiles at everyone with "Much the same smile" he does not like it. He wants her to smile at him differently because he is so much more important than anyone else. Therefore "I gave commands". Instead of speaking to his wife, the Duke orders her. The word "commands" means he treats her like a servant or slave. She is his possession to punish and order about. After this, "all smiles stopped". His wife is clearly upset.

At this point in the poem, the Duke changes his subject and asks the ambassador to stand, "Will't please you rise?" This is a caesura or break in the poetry line which suggests an abrupt change of direction. This denotes the moment when the Duchess's smiles stopped, happiness died, and, presumably, her life ended. The fact he does not tell us how she died makes us even more suspicious. A man as controlling and powerful as the Duke could easily have his wife murdered because she ceased to please him. "all smiles stopped" could hint that the Duke had his wife killed because he was jealous of the way she smiled at other men.

The Duke moves on to the business he has with the ambassador. He says the Count, the ambassador's "master" will give him a "dowry" with his "fair daughter". A "dowry" is a sum of money and goods which the father of a daughter paid to her husband in appreciation of him taking her off his hands. It is a formal arrangement which comes from the time when women were thought of as male possessions. In the modern world, this tradition is observed in weddings by the bride's father paying for the wedding and walking her down the aisle to be given away.

Frighteningly, the Duke says the Count's daughter "is my object". This makes obvious that he thinks of women as belongings – they are objectified and dehumanised. The reader is anxious about what might happen to this new wife if she does not please her husband. The Duke ends by pointing out another one of his valuable belongings, it is a sculpture. This demonstrates that the Duke is a collector of beautiful objects which he can control; his wives are just another one of these collections.

The Duke directs the ambassador to "Notice Neptune, though, Taming a sea-horse". It is another art work. Neptune is the god of the sea. He is a powerful male figure, just like the Duke. In the sculpture he is controlling a "sea-horse". These are delicate, beautiful creatures, like the Duchess. The sculpture symbolises the relationship between the Duke and women; he wants to overpower them, and make them serve him.

Because status is so important to the Duke he tells the ambassador that it was made by a famous sculptor, Claus of Innsbruck. The appearance of having the very best is so important to the Duke that he has to boast about it. He concludes by saying that the statue was "cast in bronze for me!" The poem ends with a metal, bronze, which is hard and cold, like the Duke. The exclamatory phrase "for me!" shows that the Duke only likes things which are made especially to please him. Ownership is vital to him.

POEMS WITH LOTS OF POTENTIAL COMPARISONS WITH THIS ONE

"Sonnet 116" - provides interesting comparisons as it is about a very different ideal of love.

"La Belle Dame Sans Merci" – provides excellent comparisons as it reverses the gender relationship with the man falling victim to a powerful woman.

14. Half-caste by John Agard

POET

John Agard (1949-Present)

John Agard was born in British Guyana. He is a playwright and poet. He began writing poetry while studying for his A Levels in English, French and Latin. He later taught these languages while working in a local library. He also worked as a journalist for the "Guyana Sunday Chronicle" and published two books. Agard's father moved to London and he came to join him with his partner Grace Nichols (a famous poet in her own right) in 1977. In 2012, Agard was awarded the Queen's Gold Medal for Poetry.

BACKGROUND

Agard's father is from the Caribbean, while his mother is Portuguese. This means he is mixed race. When Agard moved to Britain in 1977 he encountered the racist word "half-caste" which angered him. The poem takes issue with the prevalent use of this word in 1970s and 1980s British society.

SUMMARY

The poem responds to a person who has called the speaker "half-caste". The speaker goes on to explain to the racist the positive things in the world which are produced by mixing things. Next, he shows how ridiculous the term is by imagining his body is only half formed or "half-caste". Finally, he concludes with an invitation to the racist to come back tomorrow, this time with a whole and open mind, and find out who he really is.

ANALYSIS

The title of the poem "Half-caste" is an offensive term used to describe people of mixed race. The word "caste" comes from the Hindu class system in which individuals are born into different levels in society from which they can never escape. At the bottom of the caste system are the so-called 'untouchables' a group of individuals who, be accident of birth, are considered to be impure and with whom others refuse to associate or to employ. Thus "caste" refers to a notion of degrees of purity which have no moral or actual basis. From the 16th Century onwards, the word came to mean race or breed.

It is interesting that in Portuguese, the word "casta" means lineage or line of inheritance, while 'casto' means pure or unmixed. As Agard's mother is Portuguese, it may be that this meaning of purity also forms part of his perception of the word. By adding the prefix 'half' to 'caste' the term becomes one of abuse, suggesting that a mixed race person is only half formed, half made, and half pure. It also implies that it is acceptable to categorise other people in a 'caste' or class system which makes certain individuals superior and well-treated and others inferior and ill-treated.

The word was used, not only by racists in the 1970s, but also by people who were, possibly, ignorant of its offensive meaning. By giving the poem this title, Agard wants to shock the reader and make us think about how the words we use can hurt others.

The poem is written in free verse with no fixed rhyme scheme or rhythm. This expresses the speaker's off the cuff angry words. He just has to confront the racist. The poem is also written largely without punctuation, forming one long sentence. This also means that all the lines run on from each other, using the technique of enjambment. This could suggest that the poet is breaking the rules of modern society and doing something different by standing up for himself. It could also underline the idea that his anger has made him speak without pause.

The poem is spelt phonetically. This means many of the words are spelt in the way a person with a Caribbean accent would pronounce them. This is a really clever technique. First, it makes clear that the poet is not ashamed of who he is and what his voice sounds like. Secondly, by writing the words phonetically, the poet forces the reader to speak with his voice. This places us completely in his shoes; we cannot help but empathise with him. We are made to imagine what it feels like to be mixed race and to be called 'half-caste'.

The first line of the poem begins with "Excuse me". This gives the poem a sense of hearing the voice of a real person who is responding to an encounter which has just happened. This is dramatic and exciting. The phrase "Excuse me" is at first sight a polite term. It is almost a stereotypically British comment. However, here the term is being used to confront an implied speaker who has presumably just called the poet "half-caste" which is not a courteous thing to do. The tone of the phrase is angry and outraged. The speaker wants the racist to stop and explain his words. The speaker goes on to say "standing on one leg I'm half caste". Here the racist is being confronted with an image which shows the ignorance of his words – the idea that if the poet is 'half-caste' then he is half made or only using half his body.

In the next stanza, the poet goes on to demand that the implied speak "Explain yuself". This is a direct instruction, requiring the racist speaker to account for their words. However, the racist's voice is not allowed to reply. Cleverly, the poet silences him or her. Instead, the poet supplies an answer himself, dominating the poem and showing his superior intellect and wit. The phrase "Explain yuself" is repeated four times throughout the poem. In this way, it forms a refrain. This keeps reminding the reader that the poet is not going to give up questioning the racist. It emphasizes the relentless demand of the poet for the racist to justify the use of his offensive term.

The poet provides a series of metaphors for being mixed race which are positive and, sometimes, highly cultured. First, he says that the Spanish artist, Picasso, who is widely considered to be the greatest painter of the 20th century, produces "a half-caste canvas" when he "mix red an green". This flaunts the poet's knowledge and shows that pictures which are sold for millions of pounds in the art world are made up of mixed paints. He also compares the idea of mixing races with the famous Russian composer Tchiakovsky who "mix a black key wid a white key" to make "a half-caste symphony". Again, this shows that mixed things are not negative; they actually form the art and music which the world most loves and prizes.

The poet uses a metaphor from British weather to show that being mixed race is like the typical climate of England which is usually produced by blending clouds and sunshine. He says "England weather nearly always half-caste in fact some o dem cloud half-caste till dem overcast so spiteful dem dont want de sun pass". This image makes fun of the British obsession with the weather, showing that there is nothing more typically British than mixed, overcast days. The poet also personifies the clouds. He describes them as "spiteful". This means they are cruel and unkind. Indeed, he says they are so mean that they refuse to let the sun shine. This invites comparisons between the cruel British clouds and the mean British racists. Both of them won't allow the sun to shine or the positivity of the world to enter.

64

The anger the speaker feels erupts into the poem when he uses an exclamation and a swear word. The poet says "ah rass". "ah" is an exclamatory word which shows an outburst of emotion. Usually, "ah" also implies that the speaker is tired of something. This suggests the poet is bored and annoyed by having to educate the racist in the true value of mixed things. "rass" is a Creole term, meaning 'arse'. The expletive is in a different language to show the speaker's racial identity emerging. This suggests his personal anger, but it also underlines that the racist does not know anything about him and does not even understand his language, while the poet is able to argue eloquently in his.

The poem repeats the refrain "Explain yuself" as the speaker moves on to the final section of the verse. Now, the poet gives up trying to educate the racist through the clever imagery of mixing things, and instead pokes fun at the term "half-caste". The poet describes what a half made or half formed man might look like and uses this image to show how ludicrous the racist term is. The poet extends this metaphor, depicting the "keen half of mih ear" and the "keen half of mih eye" with which he is listening to and watching the racist. The word "keen" has two meanings; it can mean eager or enthusiastic, but it can also mean sharp. Here the poet is using both these meanings. He is letting the racist know that he is listening to and watching him with enthusiasm because, unlike the racist, he wants to find out about him. It also shows that the poet is scrutinizing the racist sharply or with great precision. This is quite intimidating. While the racist has made a snap judgement about the poet and categorised him with the term "half-caste", the poet has done the opposite. He has put the racist under a microscope to be judged and is searching to find out what kind of man he is.

The image of the half formed man is also used to show disrespect towards the racist as the poet offers him only "half a hand" to shake. This is making fun of the idea of being half formed, while also implying that he dislikes the racist so much, he won't shake his hand properly. The poet goes on to depict the logical conclusion of calling someone "half-caste" or half formed; he says that when he sleeps he "close half a eye" and dreams "half a dream", and when the "moon begin to glow" he only casts "half a shadow". This suggests how silly the notion of being half a person is. It also underlines that the term reduces a mixed race person to someone without the right to a dream or even enough substance to form a shadow on the floor.

Having educated and humiliated the racist, the poet demands that he "must come back tomorrow". This is an imperative, placing the poet in a dominant position over the racist; for all his rudeness, the racist has been mastered by the person he despises. The poet reminds the racist that next time they meet he must come with the "whole of yu eye an de whole of yu ear an de whole of yu mind". This throws back on to the racist the term "half-caste", suggesting that all the time it was actually him who was the half formed one because he only looked at the poet with half his brain. Therefore, he did not see all of him.

The final stanza of the poem concludes by telling the racist that when they meet again he will tell him "de other half of my story". Thus the poet makes clear that the racist has judged him without knowing him; this is the meaning of pre-judice. He is giving the racist a second chance to find out the whole individual.

POEMS WITH LOTS OF POTENTIAL COMPARISONS WITH THIS ONE

"Search for my Tongue" – provides interesting comparisons with an individual who feels conflicted because their identity is a mixture of two languages.

"Poem at Thirty-Nine" – provides a juxtaposition with another poetic voice who speaks defiantly and proudly about her identity.

15. "Do not go gentle into that good night" by Dylan Thomas

POET

Dylan Thomas (1914-1953)

Dylan Thomas is a famous welsh poet and writer. Born in Swansea, he began writing and publishing while a teenager. He suffered from alcoholism and led a wild and reckless life. Thomas struggled to survive financially from his poetry and so began doing reading tours and radio broadcasts for the BBC. It was these broadcasts which made him famous. He travelled to America in the 1950s to give poetry readings, but while in New York in 1953, he became ill and died at the age of 39.

BACKGROUND

The poem was written in 1951 to his dying father.

SUMMARY

The poem is an appeal from the poet to his father to fight against his impending death.

ANALYSIS

The poem is written in the form of a villanelle. This is a nineteen-line poem which has a fixed rhythm and rhyme. All villanelles have five stanzas with three lines, concluding with a quatrain of four lines. Within these verses there are set refrains or repeated lines which operate like choruses in songs. The form originated as a simple song, usually concerned with pastoral or countryside matters. However, it later became a form that dealt with obsessions. This theme is primary in Thomas's poem which relentlessly dwells on his desire for his father to resist death.

The poem begins with a line which becomes a refrain in the poem, being repeated three times. This repetition gives the poem the quality of obsession. Thomas cannot stop this thought running through his head. The opening line, "Do not go gentle into that good night" is an imperative or instruction. This makes the poem sound quite authoritative or bossy, but this is ironic. The entire poem actually pivots around the terrible irony that even if his father fights against death, it will always win. The word "gentle" is interesting here. Grammatically, the sentence should use an adverb – gently, but Thomas chooses to employ an adjective. This makes the sentence sound jarring and alerts the reader to the importance of the word. Gentle means mild, meek or calm. Here Thomas is telling his dying father not to face death passively or meekly but to fight. The "good night" is a metaphor for death. It compares death to the end of a day; importantly it is a "good" end, so death is not a terrible place. The phrase is also a pun which reminds the reader of the words we say to our parents before going to bed. This makes the emotion of losing Thomas's father even more powerful.

The poet goes on to give his opinion that "Old age should burn and rave at close of day". This means he thinks the elderly ought to fight death in a fiery, angry way. They should "rave" or speak with anger and madness against the end of their lives. He then repeats the word "rage" meaning passionately express your hatred. The repetition shows how important Thomas believes this to be. "The dying of the light" extends the metaphor of a life as a single day and suggests that dusk is the end of our lives. This line becomes a second refrain, ending stanzas one, three, four and five.

The next four stanzas are all examples of different types of men who fight against death when it approaches. They are each examples for Thomas's father to emulate or copy. The second stanza describes the deaths of "wise" or clever men. The poet says even though they know "dark is right" or death is inevitable, they still do not "go gentle". The reason they fight is "Because their words had forked no lightning". This metaphor compares the wise words of the clever men with bolts of lightning. It is because all their wisdom has not produced lightning or a powerful effect in the universe, they refuse to let death take them away. Thus it is the fact they have not made a difference in their lives which leads them to fight death. Thomas repeats this idea in stanzas two to five. It is a sad concept; he is suggesting that because none of us ever fully appreciates our life when we have it, then we must fight to keep it when death wants to take it from us.

The third stanza employs a different type of dying man as an example. This time it is a "good" man. This suggests a person who is moral and well-meaning. The poet says these men fight death because when the "last wave" goes by they see they have not made a difference. The "last wave" is a metaphor comparing life with a beach on which waves are crashing. The "last wave" is the one which marks the end of your time on the beach. These men realise at the end of their lives that their actions were "frail" or weak and ineffectual. Their moral lives "might have" or could have "danced in a green bay". This means their good deeds could have taken them from the crashing waves of the beach to a happy moment of dancing with others in the calm of a bay or sheltered part of the sea. However, because this did not happen, they must fight death.

Stanza four deals with "Wild men". These are men who have lived life to excess, drinking and enjoying themselves. They "caught and sang the sun in flight". Here their partying lives are compared to being able to catch hold of the sun, the most powerful object in the universe, and to sing with it, or be part of its exciting existence. However, facing death, the "wild men" realise or "learn" that they "grieved it on its way" or made their lives pass more quickly by enjoying themselves. Therefore they fight death.

Stanza five describes the "Grave men". There is a pun here on the word "grave". It means serious, but it also suggests the idea of death and the graves in which the dead will be buried. These serious men "see with blinding sight". This is an oxymoron, combining the apparently opposite ideas of blindness and seeing together to make the reader realise something startling. The oxymoron here suggests that "Grave men" are able to perceive the world more clearly than others. However, their penetrating eyes "could" have done much more during their lives. They have not allowed them to "blaze like meteors and be gay". This simile explains that serious men do not use their keen wits to be spectacular like falling stars, or to enjoy themselves. Therefore when they face death, they must fight it.

Thomas employs four different examples for his father of men who resist death due to regrets. Each type of man is characterised by a different elemental force, such as lightning or water or sun or meteors. These images show that lives should be lived on a grand scale, and that we should reach for the stars. If we are not able to clasp the stars then we have not fulfilled our life's potential. This is a clever technique as Thomas is making a very personal appeal to his dying father also something universal and important to everyone.

The final stanza goes back to Thomas's father and addresses him directly. The opening phrase "And you, my father" is touching. It begins the stanza with a conjunction which should normally be used to connect parts of a sentence. Here the conjunction reminds the reader that all the other things the poet has described are only parts of a picture which is being painted just for his dad. The possessive pronoun "my" underlines the fact this is very personal.

The poet goes on to imagine his father facing death through a metaphor of him standing on a mountain; he is "there on the sad height". This image places Thomas's father high up looking down on his life and sadly facing death. Thomas then starts to beg his father, instructing him to "Curse, bless, me now with your fierce tears". Therefore he doesn't care if his father swears at him or confers love with his weeping. Thomas has got to the point that he would rather his father stayed alive even if he is kept alive through bad temper or anger. The religious diction of "bless" is extended in the phrase "I pray", showing Thomas is realising that God is the only person he can appeal to now to help his father. The phrase "I pray" means both I wish and I am speaking to God.

Thomas concludes the poem by repeating his two refrains together. He tells his father once more not to die mildly and that he must fight with anger against death. The repetition of the refrains, formed here in one great summary, does not make the reader think that Thomas can win. Ironically, the fact he has not been able to move on from his instruction at the beginning of the poem, and has had to repeat it again, tells us that he is fighting a losing battle. Thus the poem describes a son's desire to keep his father from death, but his ultimate failure to do so.

POEMS WITH LOTS OF POTENTIAL COMPARISONS WITH THIS ONE

"If" – provides comparisons because it is also a poem about the relationship between a father and son.

"Prayer Before Birth" – provides lots of comparisons because it is also about a person facing a horrible event. However, in MacNeice's poem birth is more awful than death.

"Piano" – provides lots of useful comparisons because both poems are about a son thinking about a dead or dying parent.

"poem at Thirty Nine" – provides useful comparisons as both poets are writing about their dead or dying fathers.

"Remember" – provides comparisons between a poetic voice facing their own death and a poet facing the death of someone else

POET

Christina Rossetti (1830-1894)

Rossetti was the child of an Italian immigrant who lectured at King's College, London. Her father died of tuberculosis in 1854, which led to Christina's nervous breakdown and a constant financial struggle for her family. Rossetti's brother Dante Gabriel was a famous painter and founder of the Pre-Raphaelite Brotherhood Movement in art which sought to reverse the effects of industrialisation and return art to the truth of nature. Christina Rossetti was a devout Anglo Catholic who did charitable work with homeless women to educate and improve their conditions. She received two proposals of marriage during her lifetime, but refused them both due to a religious incompatibility. She remained single all her life. She suffered from Grave's Disease and later breast cancer which eventually killed her in 1894, aged 64. She wrote and published poetry from her teenage years and throughout her life.

BACKGROUND

The poem was written when Rossetti was only nineteen years old. She had already experienced profound bereavement after the death of her father when she was fourteen. The poem is in a sonnet form which comes from Italy. Her family was Italian and her father taught Italian literature and poetry at King's College.

SUMMARY

The speaker of the poem instructs her loved one to remember her when she is dead. However, by the end of the sonnet the speaker makes a different suggestion; she realises that she would rather her lover forget her and be happy, than remember her and be sad.

ANALYSIS

The poem is written in the sonnet form. The sonnet is a fourteen line poem invented in Italy in the medieval period. Traditionally, sonnets were written by aristocratic men to show off their literary skill. They were always addressed to a woman or Beloved figure. Poets would write whole sequences of sonnets which would form the scenes or episodes in a love story. At a time when novels did not exist, these poems offered extended and developing narratives. Because the form was invented in Italy, a Catholic country, the Beloved was usually given the attributes of the Virgin Mary. She would therefore be pure, moral and unwilling to enter a sexual relationship with the male poet. Rossetti takes these typical ingredients or conventions of the sonnet and adapts them. By writing a sonnet, Rossetti is entering into a tradition of male love verse; this shows that she believes women are able to speak and feel as passionately about love as men. She also adapts the subject matter of the form; although the poem is still about love, it is also about death and memory. This shows her skill as a poet, exploiting the form to create new meanings. The title of the poem "Remember" is consequently surprising for a sonnet as it is not directly about love. Instead, the title seems to speak an instruction for a listener to obey. We are not sure at this stage if the intended listener is the Beloved or the reader. It places the reader under an immediate pressure to memorise what is about to be said and to be able to recall it in the future.

The poem is a Petrarchan sonnet. This form of sonnet divides the fourteen iambic pentameter lines into two distinct sections. The first eight lines or octave rhyme ABBA ABBA, while the final six lines or sestet rhyme CDE CDE. Petrarchan sonnets take this form in order to offer an opportunity for the poem to change the direction of its thoughts at the end of the octave. This change of direction is called the volta.

The octave begins with the phrase "Remember me". This imperative is clearly addressed to a Beloved. It takes the form of an instruction. This gives the poetic voice a sense of authority and power. However, this authority is diminished when we realise that the instruction is repeated again in line five and in line seven, forming a refrain. The repetition of the order reduces its power, making the speaker seem uncertain or desperate about being heard. Moreover, the word "remember" is repeated five times in the fourteen lines of the poem. This underlines the anxiety of the speaker and possibly the sense that remembering is something which may be difficult to do.

The poem also begins with a pronoun – "me". This pronoun is rapidly followed by another one in the opening line – "I". This reiteration of words directing us back to the speaker shows how keen she is to be heard, and suggests that the subject matter of the poem is deeply personal and important to her. The first line ends with "when I am gone away." The Beloved is therefore being told to remember the speaker when they have left. The word "gone" could mean that the speaker is simply departing. However, the more morbid meaning of this is revealed in the second line when the speaker repeats "Gone far away". By breaking up the phrase with the word "far" the speaker extends the concept and this lengthening makes the distance she will go appear even greater. The line ends with a metaphor – "into the silent land". It is now clear that the speaker is not just leaving the Beloved; their journey is taking them to somewhere not human – to a realm of death. Therefore the previous phrases have been euphemisms or nicer ways of seeing something awful; they are less upsetting words for death. Death is being imagined here as a journey, a trip to be embarked upon to a distant location. The location "the silent land" is an unnerving image. It describes a world where there is no sound. A lack of sound suggests possibly that the speaker's senses will be deadened. It also implies that the afterlife is a lonely world with no one else to speak to or to hear. This could be read as quite unchristian; it is certainly not a typical view of heaven. More positively, the "silent land" could be interpreted as a place of quiet and therefore calm.

Having told her Beloved that she will die and that he must remember her, the speaker describes what it will be like when she is gone. She paints a vivid picture of the Beloved being unable to "hold me by the hand". This suggests that normally there is physical intimacy between them, but that this will be impossible after death. She also explains that she will have no alternative; "Nor I half turn to go yet turning stay". Lines three, four and five contain three negatives: "no", "Nor" and "no". These underline the inescapable nature of death, and the fact that she will not be able to control or evade it.

The speaker goes on to imagine other examples of what will be lost when she dies. The couple will not be able to share "our future that you planned" and it "will be late to counsel then or pray". This means she moves from the physical companionship they share when holding hands to the emotional and mental relationship they have. It describes a relationship which has been ended prematurely, as there was a "future" which can now not be realised. This is sad. More emotional still, is the realisation that time will run out for them, and there will be no opportunity to gain advice from friends or to seek help from God. The idea that neither the human nor the divine realms will be able to help is again disturbing and depressing. Throughout these lines, the refrain "Remember me" echoes, reminding the Beloved that the only way she can survive is in his thoughts.

The volta comes at the end of the octave with the word "Yet". This changes everything. The word is a synonym for 'but'. The speaker is offering an alternative. The reader must wonder if this alternative is being provided because the speaker has lost confidence in the Beloved remembering her or if a new idea has simply occurred.

The speaker now moves on to deal with the possibility of forgetting. This is ironic in a poem entitled "Remember". The sestet contains two "if"s. They focus the reader on the possible aftermath of the speaker's death. The speaker tells her Beloved "if you should forget me for a while And afterwards remember, do not grieve". Here she reassures the Beloved that if he does not remember her constantly and begins to live his life again that he should not feel guilty. Interestingly, she uses the word "grieve" to describe the emotion of sadness that he should not feel about forgetting her. This word is more usually applied to the feelings of a person who is remembering a dead loved one. This is ironic.

The speaker goes on to explain why she does not want her Beloved to be sad when she is gone – "For if the darkness and corruption leave A vestige of the thoughts that once I had". The "darkness and corruption" describe death itself. Again this appears quite unchristian as death is not imagined as a gateway to a heavenly afterlife. Instead, death is lacking light and it is full of decay. The word "corruption" is being used here in its archaic form to mean putrefaction or the process of becoming rotten. It is a horrible image which draws the reader's attention to the fact that the speaker's body will be decaying in the grave. However, she hopes that a "vestige" or little bit of her "thoughts" or personality will still survive after her body's destruction. This might refer to a soul living on after death or simply a spiritual presence or echo of her. The speaker believes that if a tiny part of her soul can remain when her body has decayed, that this part of her would want her Beloved to be happy.

The final two lines of the sonnet reverse the meaning of the octave. The speaker seems to have changed her mind; now she has realised that she would rather her Beloved avoids her instruction to "Remember me" if this means he can be happy without her. She says "Better by far". This emphasizes the change in her thoughts, and her acknowledgement that she would sacrifice the lasting memory of her in return for her lover's contentment. These lines juxtapose two contradictory phrases: "you should forget and smile" and "you should remember and be sad". The phrases equate forgetting with happiness and remembering with grief. It is as though the speaker of the sonnet has spent the octave thinking about her own fears of death, but has now decided that she loves her partner enough to want to be obliterated from his memory so he can be happy once again. Thus the speaker ultimately gives up on her order to "remember" and gives her Beloved permission to move on with his life after she is gone. She wants him to "smile". This simple word encapsulates the hope she has for the Beloved's future which is starkly in contrast with her own expected death, decay and eradication from memory.

POEMS WITH LOTS OF POTENTIAL COMPARISONS WITH THIS ONE

"War Photographer" – provides an interesting contrast with this poem as it is also about capturing death and destruction, but this time in photographs. The photographer wants people to notice and remember, whereas Rossetti finally decides forgetting is better.

"My Last Duchess" – provides a point of comparison between a male voice remembering a dead lover, while this poem has a female voice instructing forgetfulness of herself.

"Do not go gentle into that good night" – provides a powerful comparison as Thomas pleads with his father to fight against death, and Rossetti's speaker accepts the inevitability of death.

Printed in Great Britain
by Amazon

85128571R00045

Latin
FOR COMMON ENTRANCE

13+
LEVEL 1

Exam
Practice
Answers

R.C. Bass

GALORE
PARK

AN HACHETTE UK COMPANY

About the author

Bob Bass taught at prep schools in Somerset, Kenya and Sussex before moving in 1987 to Orwell Park, Ipswich, where he is Head of Classics and Senior Master. He has served on the editorial board of the *Journal of Classics Teaching* and on the Council of the Joint Association of Classical Teachers. For 12 years he edited the SATIPS Classics Broadsheet, and has been IAPS' Subject Leader and then Subject Adviser in Classics. He is the Chief Setter of ISEB's Common Entrance and Common Academic Scholarship Latin papers, proof-reader for their Greek papers, and an IGCSE examiner. He is the author of various Latin and Greek resources targeted at young learners.

Every effort has been made to trace all copyright holders, but if any have been inadvertently overlooked, the Publishers will be pleased to make the necessary arrangements at the first opportunity.

Although every effort has been made to ensure that website addresses are correct at time of going to press, Galore Park cannot be held responsible for the content of any website mentioned in this book. It is sometimes possible to find a relocated web page by typing in the address of the home page for a website in the URL window of your browser.

Hachette UK's policy is to use papers that are natural, renewable and recyclable products and made from wood grown in sustainable forests. The logging and manufacturing processes are expected to conform to the environmental regulations of the country of origin.

Orders: please contact Bookpoint Ltd, 130 Milton Park, Abingdon, Oxon OX14 4SB. Telephone: (44) 01235 827720. Fax: (44) 01235 400454. Email education@bookpoint.co.uk Lines are open from 9 a.m. to 5 p.m., Monday to Saturday, with a 24-hour message answering service. Visit our website at www.galorepark.co.uk for details of other revision guides for Common Entrance, examination papers and Galore Park publications.

ISBN: 978 1 471853 46 3

© Robert C. Bass 2015

First published in 2015 by
Galore Park Publishing Ltd,
An Hachette UK Company
Carmelite House
50 Victoria Embankment
London EC4Y 0DZ
www.galorepark.co.uk

Impression number 10 9 8 7 6 5 4 3 2

Year 2019 2018 2017

Typeset in India

Printed in the United Kingdom

A catalogue record for this title is available from the British Library.

Contents

Introduction

A note on translation into English

The present tense in Latin may be translated using either of two aspects: the present simple (amo = I love) or the present continuous/progressive (amo = I am loving).

The imperfect tense may be translated as either amabam = I was loving or amabam = I used to love.

The perfect tense may be translated as the past preterite or aorist (amavi = I loved) or the present perfect (amavi = I have loved).

This answer book tends to use whichever makes the most sense in the context of the piece. Pupils should not (at this stage) be penalised for using a form that, while grammatically correct, is not given as the example answer in this book.

The syllabus and your exams

For Common Entrance Latin, you will sit an exam lasting one hour. You will choose one of the three levels, Level 1, Level 2 or Level 3, as agreed with your teacher.

The format of each level is the same, but the material gets harder. In each level, there are four questions worth a total of 75 marks, as follows:

Question 1 (15 marks)

A short passage of Latin will be set, on which you will be asked to answer eight to ten questions, testing your understanding of the passage. You will not be expected to write a translation of the passage, but clearly you need to have translated it in your head, in order to answer the questions.

Question 2 (30 marks)

Another, slightly longer passage will be set, continuing the story from the passage in Question 1. You will be asked to translate this passage, writing your translation on alternate lines.

Question 3 (20 marks)

Another short passage of Latin will be set, continuing the story from the earlier two passages. Questions will be set, testing your knowledge of Latin grammar and how the language works. You will not be asked to translate this passage, but again you will find it difficult to answer the questions unless you have translated it for yourself.

The questions will fall into the following types:

- From the passage give, in Latin, one example of: (an adjective, a preposition followed by the accusative, a noun in the genitive, a verb in the imperfect tense, etc.)

- **erat** (line 2). In which tense is this verb? What is the 1st person singular of the present tense of this verb?

- **pueros** (line 4). In which case is this noun? Why is this case used?

- **vocaverunt** (line 5). What does this word mean? What is the connection between **vocaverunt** and the English word *vocation*?

- **necat** (line 5) means *he kills*. How would you say in Latin *he was killing* (imperfect tense)?

And last but not least:

- Using the vocabulary given, translate the following two short sentences into Latin.

Most candidates lose the majority of their marks on Question 3 by falling into the trap of thinking they do not need to translate the passage. They simply guess the answers. To answer a question such as 'in which case is the word **templum** in line 3?', you have to have translated the sentence in which the word **templum** is. Otherwise you will simply be guessing, particularly with a word such as **templum**, which could be any of nominative, vocative or accusative singular.

Question 4 (10 marks)

You will be set eight questions on four areas: Roman domestic life; the city of Rome; the army and Roman Britain; and Greek mythology. Each question will have two parts, part (i) and part (ii). You select **one** question, and answer both parts of it. Examples are given below:

The city of Rome

(c) (i) Tell the story of Cloelia.

(ii) Which elements of this story would the Romans have found particularly admirable? Explain your answer.

Greek mythology

(h) (i) Tell the story of Odysseus' encounter with the Cyclops.

(ii) Describe two qualities which Odysseus displayed in this encounter.

These are two of the eight questions that might have been set, labelled (a) to (h). If you had chosen to do the one labelled (c) above, you would have done both part (i) and part (ii) of that question.

Tips on revising

Get the best out of your brain

- Give your brain plenty of oxygen by exercising. You can only revise effectively if you feel fit and well.
- Eat healthy food while you are revising. Your brain works better when you give it good fuel.
- Think positively. Give your brain positive messages so that it will want to study.
- Keep calm. If your brain is stressed, it will not operate effectively.
- Take regular breaks during your study time.
- Get enough sleep. Your brain will carry on sorting out what you have revised while you sleep.

Get the most from your revision

- Don't work for hours without a break. Revise for 20–30 minutes, then take a five-minute break.
- Do good things in your breaks: listen to your favourite music, eat healthy food, drink some water, do some exercise or juggle. Don't read a book, watch TV or play on the computer; it will conflict with what your brain is trying to learn.
- When you go back to your revision, review what you have just learnt.
- Regularly review the material you have learnt.

Get motivated

- Set yourself some goals and promise yourself a treat when the exams are over.
- Make the most of all the expertise and talent available to you at school and at home. If you don't understand something, ask your teacher to explain.

- Get organised. Find a quiet place to revise and make sure you have all the equipment you need.

- Use year and weekly planners to help you organise your time so that you revise all subjects equally. (Available for download from www.galorepark.co.uk)

- Use topic and subject checklists to help you keep on top of what you are revising. (Available for download from www.galorepark.co.uk)

Know what to expect in the exam

- Use past papers to familiarise yourself with the format of the exam.

- Make sure you understand the language examiners use.

Before the exam

- Have all your equipment and pens ready the night before.

- Make sure you are at your best by getting a good night's sleep before the exam.

- Have a good breakfast in the morning.

- Take some water into the exam if you are allowed.

- Think positively and keep calm.

During the exam

- Have a watch on your desk. Work out how much time you need to allocate to each question and try to stick to it.

- Make sure you read and understand the instructions on the front of the exam paper.

- Allow some time at the start to read and consider the questions carefully before writing anything.

- Read every question at least twice. Don't rush into answering before you have a chance to think about it.

1

Exercise 1.1

1 The Romans used to speak Latin.

2 Rome was situated in Latium.

3 Rome stands on the River Tiber.

4 The large area controlled by Rome was called the Roman Empire.

5 These are called Romance languages.

1 mark for each question. Total: 5

Exercise 1.2

1 amat.

2 ambulas.

3 clamant.

4 intramus.

5 parant.

6 ambulant.

7 pugnamus.

8 festino.

9 portat.

10 habitatis.

11 laborat.

12 cantamus.

13 pugnas.

14 ambulat.

15 portant.

16 porto.

17 clamas.

18 habitant.

19 amat.

20 laborat.

21 festinant.

22 festinant.

23 pugnat.

24 amamus.

25 laborant.

26 habito.

27 cantant.

28 intrat.

29 intratis.

30 portatis.

31 ambulo.

32 clamat.

33 paratis.

34 pugnant.

35 amant.

36 laboramus.

37 cantatis.

38 intrant.

39 festinat.

40 habitamus.

1 mark for each question. Total: 40

Exercise 1.3

1 amas.

2 intramus.

3 portant.

4 habitat.

5 clamatis.

6 ambulamus.

7 ambulo.

8 laborant.

9 parat.

10 festinas.

11 pugnant.

12 cantamus.

13 laboro.

14 cantant.

15 pugnatis.

1 mark for each question. Total: 1

Exercise 1.4

1 amamus.

2 habitas.

3 laboramus.

4 cantamus.

5 ambulat.

6 clamas.

7 portamus.

8 intratis.

9 canto.

10 pugnamus.

11 parant.

12 festinant.

13 paras.

14 portatis.

15 festinat.

1 mark for each question. Total: 15

Exercise 1.5

1 I carry.

2 He/She/It enters.

3 They live.

4 I prepare.

5 You love.

6 You live.

7 You enter.

8 I work.

9 We sing.

10 You work.

11 You sing.

12 We live.

13 He/She/It shouts.

14 They hurry.

15 You shout.

16 You prepare.

17 He/She/It lives.

18 We fight.

19 They work.

20 They walk.

Chapter 1

21 You live.

22 We prepare.

23 You work.

24 You fight.

25 I live.

26 He/She/It prepares.

27 He/She/It fights.

28 You hurry.

29 You walk.

30 We hurry.

31 They carry.

32 We enter.

33 He/She/It works.

34 You prepare.

35 You fight

36 You carry.

37 You enter.

38 I hurry.

39 They sing.

40 We carry.

41 They enter.

42 You hurry.

43 I shout.

44 We work.

45 They prepare.

46 He/She/It carries.

47 I walk.

48 He/She/It hurries.

49 You walk.

50 You carry.

1 mark for each question. Total: 50

Exercise 1.6

1 3rd person plural.

2 3rd person singular.

3 2nd person plural.

4 2nd person singular.

5 1st person plural.

6 3rd person plural.

7 2nd person singular.

8 2nd person plural.

9 3rd person singular.

10 3rd person plural.

2 marks for each question. Total: 20

Exercise 1.7

1 2nd person plural.

2 2nd person singular.

3 3rd person plural.

4 1st person plural.

5 3rd person singular.

6 3rd person singular.

7 3rd person plural.

8 2nd person plural.

9 2nd person singular.

10 3rd person singular.

2 marks for each question. Total: 20

Exercise 1.8

1 cantas.

2 cantatis.

3 laboramus.

4 clamant.

5 ambulat.

6 portas.

7 festinamus.

8 parant.

9 habitatis.

10 intrat.

1 mark for each question. Total: 10

Exercise 1.9

1 ambulas et cantas.

2 clamant et laborant.

3 canto et festino.

4 habitant et pugnant.

5 laboramus et paramus.

6 cantant et clamant.

7 intratis et clamatis.

8 clamat et cantat.

9 habitant et laborant.

10 clamamus et festinamus.

2 marks for each question. Total: 20

Exercise 1.10

1 We live and work.

2 They shout and fight.

3 You walk and shout.

4 You walk and sing.

5 They hurry and prepare.

6 I sing and shout.

7 He shouts and sings.

8 We enter and prepare.

9 You fight and live.

10 They sing and shout.

2 marks for each question. Total: 20

Exercise 2.1

1 Marcus cantat.

2 Marcus et Sextus cantant.

3 Aurelia pugnat.

4 Flavia laborat.

5 Iulia et Flavia festinant.

6 Marcus clamat.

7 Sextus et Flavia pugnant.

8 Aurelia intrat.

9 Cornelius et Publius clamant.

10 Valeria festinat.

1 mark for each question. Total: 10

Exercise 2.2

1 Marcus hurries.

2 Flavia shouts.

3 Valeria sings.

4 Sextus walks.

5 Aurelia works.

6 Julia works.

7 Aurelia and Julia work.

8 Cornelius fights.

9 Publius fights.

10 Cornelius and Publius fight.

11 Flavia and Julia enter.

12 Marcus works.

13 Julia sings.

14 Cornelius and Publius walk.

15 Valeria walks.

1 mark for each question. Total: 15

Exercise 2.3

1 Marcus pugnat.

2 Sextus pugnat.

3 Marcus et Sextus pugnant.

4 Flavia laborat.

5 Aurelia laborat.

6 Flavia et Aurelia laborant.

7 Cornelius et Publius clamant.

8 Iulia festinat.

9 Aurelia et Flavia cantant.

10 Marcus ambulat.

2 marks for each question. Total: 20

Exercise 2.4

1 I see.

2 I do not see.

3 I warn.

4 Marcus stays.

5 We see.

6 They have.

7 Aurelia and Valeria stay.

8 I do not warn.

9 I see and stay.

10 We have.

11 You warn.

12 You see.

13 Julia stays.

14 We do not see.

15 We warn.

16 You stay.

17 Marcus and Sextus do not stay.

18 I have.

19 Flavia sees.

20 Julia does not see.

1 mark for each question. Total: 20

Exercise 2.5

1 manet.

2 non manet.

3 monemus.

4 vides.

5 manent.

6 habet.

7 habeo.

8 video et maneo.

9 Marcus monet.

10 Sextus non monet.

11 Cornelius et Publius manent.

12 non vident.

13 monetis.

14 videt.

15 videmus.

16 non moneo.

17 monet.

18 non habes.

19 manent et vident.

20 videt.

1 mark for each question. Total: 20

Exercise 2.6

(clamo)

clamas

(clamat)

clamamus

(clamatis)

clamant

habeo

habes

habet

habemus

habetis

(habent)

maneo

manes

(manet)

manemus

manetis

manent

laboro

(laboras)

laborat

laboramus

laboratis

laborant

canto

cantas

cantat

cantamus

cantatis

cantant

video

vides

videt

videmus

videtis

vident

1 mark for each question. Total: 30

Exercise 2.7

1 amamus. (1)

2 vident. (1)

3 habes. (1)

4 pugno. (1)

5 manemus et cantamus. (2)

6 Marcus videt. (1)

7 Aurelia et Valeria pugnant et clamant. (2)

8 non video. (1)

9 ambulamus et videmus. (2)

10 paramus. (1)

11 monemus. (1)

12 non monetis. (1)

13 Flavia cantat. (1)

14 Sextus monet. (1)

15 clamo et pugno. (2)

16 manet. (1)

Total: 20

Exercise 2.8

1 ambulas. (1)

2 ambulamus et videmus. (2)

3 non video. (1)

4 non vident. (1)

5 portatis. (1)

6 manent. (1)

7 pugnas. (1)

8 videmus et monemus. (2)

9 non festinat. (1)

10 non ambulamus. (1)

11 monetis. (1)

12 cantat. (1)

13 vides. (1)

14 non portant. (1)

15 clamamus. (1)

16 videtis et manetis. (2)

17 manent et cantant. (2)

18 Flavia videt et clamat. (3)

19 non maneo. (2)

20 Sextus et Publius manent et pugnant. (4)

Total: 30

Exercise 2.9

1 monet.	He warns.
2 amat.	He loves.
3 videmus.	We see.
4 clamant.	They shout.
5 manetis.	You stay.
6 habes.	You have.
7 festino.	I hurry.
8 portas.	You carry.
9 paratis.	You prepare.
10 manet.	He stays.

2 marks for each question. Total: 20

Exercise 2.10

1 We love.	1st person	Plural
2 You warn.	2nd person	Plural
3 You sing.	2nd person	Singular
4 We see.	1st person	Plural
5 You shout.	2nd person	Plural
6 He stays.	3rd person	Singular
7 They walk.	3rd person	Plural
8 I have.	1st person	Singular
9 He fights.	3rd person	Singular
10 They prepare.	3rd person	Plural

3 marks for each question. Total: 30

Exercise 3.1

1	nautae	sailors
2	agricolae	farmers
3	feminae	women
4	insulae	islands
5	viae	roads
6	filiae	daughters
7	sagittae	arrows
8	portae	gates
9	poetae	poets
10	undae	waves

2 marks for each question. Total: 20

Exercise 3.2

1 puella cantat. (2)

2 puellae cantant. (2)

3 nauta videt. (2)

4 nautae vident. (2)

5 Cornelius laborat. (2)

6 Cornelius et Flavia clamant. (3)

7 nauta clamat. (2)

8 feminae ambulant. (2)

9 filia festinat. (2)

10 nautae laborant. (2)

11 Publius intrat. (2)

12 filiae monent. (2)

13 puella manet. (2)

14 puellae manent. (2)

15 Valerius monet. (2)

16 puellae manent et cantant. (3)

17 agricola et filia manent. (3)

18 monemus. (1)

19 habes. (1)

20 video. (1)

Total: 40

Exercise 3.3

1 The girl is shouting.

2 The girls are shouting.

3 The woman sees.

4 The women see.

5 The farmer hurries.

6 Flavia warns.

7 The sailors are fighting.

8 The daughter is walking.

9 The farmers are staying.

10 Cornelius is warning.

2 marks for each question. Total: 20

Exercise 3.4

1 The daughters are singing. (2)

2 The sailors are hurrying. (2)

3 The farmers are warning. (2)

4 The woman sees. (2)

5 The farmer is working. (2)

6 The farmers are working and shouting. (3)

7 The girls are shouting and singing. (3)

8 Publius stays and sees. (3)

9 The sailor is shouting and fighting. (3)

10 The girls and women are hurrying. (3)

Total: 25

Exercise 4.1

1 The girl (subject) likes the farmer (object).

2 The farmer (subject) likes the girl (object).

3 The teacher (subject) punishes the pupil (object).

4 The cat (subject) is chasing the mouse (object).

5 The man (subject) is looking at the woman (object).

2 marks for each question. Total: 10

Exercise 4.2

1 agricolam

2 deam

3 nautam

4 feminam

5 filiam

1 mark for each question. Total: 5

Exercise 4.3

1 The girl loves the sailor.

2 The sailor loves the girl.

3 The farmer loves the daughter.

4 The daughter loves the farmer.

5 The farmer loves the woman.

6 The woman loves the farmer.

7 The sailor loves the woman.

8 The woman does not love the sailor.

9 The farmer loves the sailor.

10 The sailor loves the farmer.

3 marks for each question. Total: 30

Exercise 4.4

1 The farmer has a spear.

2 The farmer holds a spear.

3 The farmer loves the spear.

4 The sailor loves money.

5 The girl praises the queen.

6 The farmer looks at the queen.

7 The queen has a daughter.

8 The queen loves her daughter.

9 The farmer calls his daughter.

10 The queen sees the goddess.

3 marks for each question. Total: 30

Exercise 4.5

1 (a) puella amat agricolam. (3)

  (b) puella agricolam amat. (1)

2 (a) agricola amat puellam. (3)

  (b) agricola puellam amat. (1)

3 (a) regina amat pecuniam. (3)

  (b) regina pecuniam amat. (1)

4 (a) femina laudat deam. (3)

  (b) femina deam laudat. (1)

5 (a) nauta habet hastam. (3)

  (b) nauta hastam habet. (1)

6 (a) Flavia spectat pecuniam. (3)

  (b) Flavia pecuniam spectat. (1)

7 (a) regina habet filiam. (3)

  (b) regina filiam habet. (1)

8 (a) puella necat reginam. (3)

  (b) puella reginam necat. (1)

9 (a) dea monet reginam. (3)

  (b) dea reginam monet. (1)

10 (a) regina amat nautam. (3)

  (b) regina nautam amat. (1)

3+1 marks for each question. Total: 40

Exercise 5.1

Flavia is walking.(2) Flavia is walking in the street.(3) Flavia is walking and singing.(3)

A sailor is walking.(2) The sailor is walking in the street.(3) The sailor is not singing.(3) The sailor sees Flavia.(3) The sailor looks at Flavia.(3) The sailor likes Flavia.(3)

Flavia sees the sailor.(3) Flavia looks at the sailor.(3) Flavia likes the sailor.(3) Flavia is happy.(3) The sailor is happy.(3)

Total: 40

Exercise 5.2

1 ambulat (lines 1/2/3)/cantat (lines 2/4)/spectat (lines 5/6)/amat (lines 5/7).   (1)

2 videt (lines 4/6).   (1)

3 3rd.   (1)

4 video.   (1)

5 *spectat* means 'he looks at', and spectacles help you to look at things.   (2)

Total: 6

Exercise 5.3

1 You sing.

2 We laugh.

3 They hold.

4 They hurry.

5 He calls.

6 You see.

7 You walk.

8 We warn.

9 I do not work.

10 He has.

1 mark for each question. Total: 10

Exercise 5.4

1 necamus.

2 tenes.

3 laborant.

4 non video.

5 habetis.

6 monet.

7 vocant.

8 manent.

9 spectamus.

10 tenet.

1 mark for each question. Total: 10

Exercise 5.5

1 The queen is laughing.

2 The girls are laughing.

3 The farmers are working.

4 The goddess is shouting.

5 The sailor is staying.

2 marks for each question. Total: 10

Exercise 5.6

1 puella ambulat.

2 puellae ambulant.

3 hastae necant.

4 feminae rident.

5 regina videt.

2 marks for each question. Total: 10

Exercise 5.7

1 The farmer is holding a spear.

2 The queen has a daughter.

3 The sailor sees the girl.

4 The girl praises the goddess.

5 The girls praise the goddess.

3 marks for each question. Total: 15

Exercise 5.8

1 puella reginam amat.

2 nauta hastam amat.

3 dea feminam monet.

4 agricola pecuniam amat.

5 agricolae pecuniam amant.

3 marks for each question. Total: 15

Exercise 5.9

1 I hold. (1)

2 I hold money. (2)

3 We see. (1)

4 We see the farmer. (2)

5 They kill. (1)

6 They kill the woman. (2)

7 You watch. (1)

8 You watch the girl. (2)

9 He praises. (1)

10 He praises the goddess. (2)

Total: 15

Exercise 5.10

1 The sailor kills.

2 He kills the sailor.

3 The queen calls.

4 He calls the queen.

5 The daughter sees.

6 He sees the daughter.

7 The girl laughs.

8 He carries money.

9 We like the spear.

10 They like money.

2 marks for each question. Total: 20

Exercise 5.11

1 pecuniam amo.

2 reginam videmus.

3 puellam portant.

4 deam vocas.

5 non rident.

6 hastam tenet.

7 nautam amatis.

8 agricolam necat.

9 feminam laudo.

10 filiam videmus.

2 marks for each question. Total: 20

Exercise 5.12

1 Marcus is laughing. (1)

2 Why is Marcus laughing? (2)

3 Marcus is laughing because he is not working. (3)

4 The sailor has a spear. (3)

5 Why does the sailor have a spear? (4)

6 The sailor has a spear because he is fighting. (5)

7 The girl loves the sailor. (3)

8 Why does the girl love the sailor? (4)

9 The girl loves the sailor because the sailor has money. (7)

10 The woman is afraid of the farmer. (3)

11 Why is the woman afraid of the farmer? (4)

12 The woman is afraid of the farmer because he is carrying a spear. (6)

Total: 45

Exercise 5.13

1 Julia is afraid of Flavia. (3)

2 Why is Julia afraid of Flavia? (4)

3 Julia is afraid of Flavia because Flavia frightens Julia. (7)

4 The farmer kills the queen. (3)

5 Why does the farmer kill the queen? (4)

6 The farmer kills the queen because he does not like the queen. (7)

7 Publius frightens the girl. (3)

8 Why does Publius frighten the girl? (4)

9 Publius frightens the girl because he does not like the girl. (7)

10 The girls are looking at the farmer. (3)

11 Why are the girls looking at the farmer? (4)

12 The girls are looking at the farmer because they like the farmer. (6)

Total: 55

Exercise 5.14

1 puellae	girls
2 feminae	women
3 reginae	queens
4 agricolae	farmers
5 nautae	sailors

2 marks for each question. Total: 10

Exercise 5.15

1 filia	daughter
2 dea	goddess
3 hasta	spear
4 nauta	sailor
5 puella	girl

2 marks for each question. Total: 10

Exercise 5.16

1 videtis.	You see.
2 clamant.	They shout.
3 habitant.	They live.
4 manemus.	We stay.
5 necatis.	You kill.

2 marks for each question. Total: 10

Exercise 5.17

| 1 canto. | I sing. |
| 2 necas. | You kill. |

3 habeo.   I have.
4 monet.   He warns.
5 terres.   You frighten.

Exercise 5.18

1 puellae laborant.   The girls are working.
2 puellae vident.   The girls see.
3 feminae monent.   The women are warning.
4 feminae festinant.   The women are hurrying.
5 nautae intrant.   The sailors are entering.

Exercise 5.19

1 hasta necat.   The spear kills.
2 regina ridet.   The queen laughs.
3 nauta manet.   The sailor stays.
4 dea vocat.   The goddess calls.
5 filia manet.   The daughter stays.

Exercise 5.20

1 puellae ambulant.   The girls are walking.
2 hastae necant.   The spears kill.
3 deae rident.   The goddesses are laughing.
4 nautae festinant.   The sailors hurry.
5 filiae manent.   The daughters are staying.

Exercise 5.21

1 femina cantat.   The woman is singing.
2 regina videt.   The queen sees.
3 puella ridet.   The girl is laughing.
4 agricola necat.   The farmer is killing.
5 nauta portat.   The sailor is carrying.

Exercise 6.1

Marcus is a sailor.(3) He is walking in the street.(2) Flavia is a girl.(3) Flavia is also walking in the street.(4) Flavia is hurrying.(2) She is hurrying to the villa.(2)

Marcus sees Flavia.(3) He likes Flavia.(2) He hurries towards Flavia.(3) He asks Flavia:(2) 'Why are you hurrying, girl?'(3)

Flavia looks at the sailor.(3) She likes the sailor.(2) She replies: 'Hello, sailor.(2) I am Flavia.(2) I am hurrying because I am preparing dinner.'(3)

Marcus asks Flavia:(3) 'Where do you live, Flavia?'(3)

Flavia replies:(2) 'I live in a villa.(3) I am preparing dinner in the villa.'(3)

Flavia invites Marcus to dinner.(3) Marcus is happy.(2) 'Great!' he replies.(2)

Flavia and Marcus hurry to the villa.(4)

Total: 66

Exercise 6.2

1	3rd.	(1)
2	Marcus.	(1)
3	Plural	(1)
4	You live. Habitat/Inhabitant	(2)

Total: 5

Exercise 6.3

1 The girl warns the sailor.

2 The girl warns the sailors.

3 The girls warn the sailor.

4 The girls warn the sailors.

5 The woman loves the farmer.

6 The woman loves the farmers.

7 The women love the farmer.

8 The women love the farmers.

9 The girls love dinner.

10 The farmer looks at the girls.

3 marks for each question. Total: 30

Exercise 6.4

1 The farmers are looking at the girl.

2 The woman is preparing dinner.

3 The queen praises the goddess.

4 The women are calling the girls.

5 The sailor has a villa.

6 Girls do not carry spears.

7 Women are afraid of farmers.

8 The sailor sees the money.

9 The farmers do not praise the goddess.

10 The women are preparing dinner.

3 marks for each question. Total: 30

Exercise 6.5

1 puella agricolam amat.

2 puellae agricolam amant.

3 puella agricolas amat.

4 puellae agricolas amant.

5 agricolae puellam spectant.

6 agricolae puellas spectant.

7 regina villam habet.

8 nauta villas spectat.

9 feminae nautas vident.

10 nautae feminas vident.

3 marks for each question. Total: 30

Exercise 6.6

1 nautae puellas spectant.

2 puella cenam parat.

3 feminae villas amant.

4 dea villam amat.

5 regina nautas vocat.

6 puellae deam laudant.

7 feminae nautas timent.

8 nautae feminas terrent.

9 dea reginam vocat.

10 puellae nautas spectant.

3 marks for each question. Total: 30

Exercise 6.7

1 I love money.

2 We are looking at the girls.

3 You see the villa.

4 They are preparing dinner.

5 The girl stays.

6 They are looking at villas.

7 We enter the villa.

8 You see the farmer.

9 I move the spear.

10 The sailors are not fighting.

2 marks for each question. Total: 20

Exercise 6.8

1 You call the farmer.

2 We have dinner.

3 The farmers are watching.

4 I have a daughter.

5 They love the girls.

6 We praise the goddess.

7 I see the villa.

8 You like women.

9 The farmers are not working.

10 We praise the dinner.

2 marks for each question. Total: 20

Exercise 6.9

1 puellas amo.
2 puellam amo.
3 cenam parant.
4 villam habet.
5 feminas vocamus.

6 agricolas videmus.
7 nautae pugnant.
8 hastam movet.
9 hastas movent.
10 deam laudo.

2 marks for each question. Total: 20

Exercise 6.10

1 cenam spectant.
2 villas amas.
3 feminam monet.
4 feminas monet.
5 deam timetis.

6 puellas amant.
7 villam habeo.
8 puellae non pugnant.
9 agricolas amas.
10 cenam parat.

2 marks for each question. Total: 20

Exercise 6.11

1 portamus.   We carry.
2 video.   I see.
3 vocas.   You call.
4 necatis.   You kill.
5 laudat.   He praises.
6 tenent.   They hold.
7 terretis.   You frighten.
8 timemus.   We fear.
9 rogas.   You ask.
10 respondet.   He replies.

2 marks for each question. Total: 20

Exercise 6.12

1 We reply.	1st person	Plural
2 You ask.	2nd person	Singular
3 I frighten.	1st person	Singular
4 You fear.	2nd person	Plural
5 You praise.	2nd person	Singular

6	They hold.	3rd person	Plural
7	He kills.	3rd person	Plural
8	We watch.	1st person	Plural
9	They laugh.	3rd person	Plural
10	You call.	2nd person	Singular

3 marks for each question. Total: 30

Exercise 7.1

Marcus and Flavia hurry to the villa.(3) Finally they enter the villa.(3) Who is working?(2) Flavia is working.(2) She is preparing dinner.(2) She is preparing a good dinner.(3) While Flavia prepares dinner,(3) Marcus sits.(2) He drinks wine.(2) Marcus likes wine.(2) Finally dinner is ready.(4) Flavia sits near Marcus.(4) They eat dinner(2) and drink wine.(3) Dinner is good.(3) Because dinner is good,(4) Marcus praises the dinner.(3)

Marcus also praises Flavia(4) because the dinner is good.(3) 'I like the wine',(2) says Marcus.(2) 'The wine is good.(3) I like the dinner.(2) The dinner is also good.'(4)

Marcus drinks wine again.(4) Flavia looks at Marcus.(3) 'You are a good girl,'(3) says Marcus.(2) Flavia does not reply,(3) but laughs.(2) Then she blushes.(2)

Total: 85

Exercise 7.2

1 Singular.	(1)
2 3rd.	(1)
3 cenam.	(1)
4 specto.	(1)
5 He laughs. Ridiculous/ridicule.	(2)

Total: 6

Exercise 7.3

1 The farmers are shouting.	(2)
2 The farmers are fighting.	(2)
3 The farmers are shouting and fighting.	(3)
4 He sits.	(1)
5 He works.	(1)
6 He does not work.	(2)
7 The girls are laughing.	(2)
8 The girls are singing.	(2)
9 The girls are laughing and singing.	(4)

10 They are not singing. (2)

11 They are afraid. (1)

12 They are singing but they are afraid. (3)

13 We watch. (1)

14 We laugh. (1)

15 We watch and laugh. (3)

Total: 30

Exercise 7.4

1 I am a girl. (2)

2 She is a woman. (2)

3 You are a sailor. (2)

4 We are farmers. (2)

5 You are goddesses. (2)

6 They are girls. (2)

7 Who are you? (2)

8 I am the queen. (2)

9 Flavia is a girl. (3)

10 Flavia and Julia are not sailors. (6)

Total: 25

Exercise 7.5

1 agricola sum. (2)

2 feminae sumus. (2)

3 regina es. (2)

4 Flavia est. (2)

5 nautae estis. (2)

6 puellae sunt. (2)

7 agricola est. (2)

8 Marcus nauta est. (3)

9 Marcus et Sextus nautae sunt. (4)

10 Flavia nauta non est. (4)

Total: 25

Exercise 7.6

1 Flavia is a Roman.

2 Flavia and Julia are Romans.

3 Marcus is a Roman.

4 Marcus and Sextus are Romans.

5 Flavia is not Greek.

6 Flavia and Julia are not Greek.

7 Marcus is not Greek.

8 Marcus and Sextus are not Greek.

9 I am a Greek girl.

10 We are Greek girls.

3 marks for each question. Total: 30

Exercise 7.7

1 We are Roman sailors. (3)

2 Marcus is a Roman sailor. (3)

3 You are a Greek girl. (3)

4 The girls are Roman. (3)

5 Flavia is a Roman girl. (3)

6 Flavia and Julia are Roman girls. (4)

7 We are Greeks. (2)

8 They are not Romans. (3)

9 Flavia is a woman. (3)

10 Flavia is not Greek. (3)

Total: 30

Exercise 7.8

1 Romanus non est. (3)

2 Romana est. (2)

3 Iulia Graeca non est. (4)

4 Marcus Graecus non est. (4)

5 Romani sumus. (2)

6 Graeci non sumus. (3)

7 Publius Romanus est. (3)

8 Romanus sum. (2)

9 agricola Romanus sum. (3)

10 Iulia Romana non est. (4)

Total: 30

Exercise 7.9

1 Marcus Romanus est. (3)

2 Marcus et Sextus Romani sunt. (5)

3 Marcus nauta Romanus est. (4)

4 Marcus nauta Graecus non est. (5)

5 Romani non sumus. (3)

6 puella Romana est. (3)

7 Graeca non est. (3)

8 puella Graeca es. (3)

9 puellae Graecae estis. (3)

10 Publius Graecus est. (3)

Total: 35

Exercise 8.1

Marcus is a Roman sailor.(4) Flavia is a Roman girl.(4) Marcus and Flavia are in the villa.(4) They are eating dinner(2) and drinking wine.(3) The dinner is good.(3) Marcus likes the dinner.(3) The wine is also good.(3) Marcus also likes the wine.(3)

Marcus praises the dinner(3) because the dinner is good.(4) Marcus also praises Flavia(4) because Flavia is a good girl.(4) Because Marcus praises Flavia,(4) Flavia blushes.(2)

Marcus sits near Flavia.(4) Marcus looks at Flavia.(3) Marcus looks at Flavia for a long time.(4) He loves Flavia.(2) Flavia sits near Marcus.(4) Flavia looks at Marcus.(3) Flavia looks at Marcus for a long time.(4) She loves Marcus.(2)

Finally Marcus says, 'I love you, Flavia.(6) Do you love me, Flavia?'(3) Flavia replies,(2) 'I love you too, Marcus!'(4)

Then Flavia kisses Marcus.(4) Now Marcus blushes.(3) He loves Flavia.(2)

Total: 100

Exercise 8.2

1 (i)   3rd.

  (ii) Plural.

  (iii) sum.   (3)

2 A conjunction.   (1)

3 Flavia.   (1)

Total: 5

Exercise 8.3

1 regunt.   10 faciunt.

2 ducis.   11 capiunt.

3 audit.   12 dicunt.

4 dormit.   13 mittimus.

5 facimus.   14 venio.

6 ponitis.   15 regis.

7 currit.   16 mittunt.

8 currimus.   17 dormiunt.

9 facitis.   18 facio.

19 currimus.

20 dicis.

21 mittimus.

22 audimus.

23 venimus.

24 venit.

25 ducunt.

26 audio.

27 ponunt.

28 non curro.

29 capit.

30 dormitis.

Exercise 8.4

1 I send.

2 You run.

3 They run.

4 I rule.

5 You sleep.

6 You lead.

7 He sends.

8 We come.

9 They lead.

10 We hear.

11 You hear.

12 You come.

13 We send.

14 They do.

15 You take.

16 They hear.

17 They sleep.

18 You send.

19 He takes.

20 You do.

21 You rule.

22 They come.

23 We lead.

24 He puts.

25 He rules.

26 He hears.

27 You put.

28 We take.

29 We run.

30 He says.

1 mark for each question. Total: 30

Exercise 8.5

1 The girl is not working. She is sleeping. (3)

2 The women take the money. (3)

3 Why are you running, girl? (3)

4 I am running because I am hurrying. (3)

5 The girl listens to the queen. (3)

6 The sailors are running. (2)

7 Why is Marcus afraid? (3)

8 Marcus is afraid because Publius is coming. (5)

9 The farmer sees the woman. (3)

10 The farmer takes the money. (3)

11 The farmer is running. (2)

12 The Romans are coming! (2)

13 Why are you working, sailors? (3)

14 We are working because we are making a villa. (4)

15 Girls like villas. (3)

Total: 45

Exercise 8.6

1 agricola deam audit. (3)

2 nautae pecuniam amant. (3)

3 Romani regunt. (2)

4 puella venit. (2)

5 femina pecuniam capit. (3)

6 cenam facimus. (2)

7 pecuniam capis. (2)

8 agricolam audio. (2)

9 cenam non amo. (3)

10 agricola filiam ducit. (3)

Total: 25

Exercise 8.7

1 adnutamus.

2 emungit.

3 torrent.

4 mico.

5 luget.

6 sorbes.

7 tergent.

8 fulcimus.

9 frenditis.

10 adolescimus.

11 praecutit.

12 angis.

13 plico.

14 molunt.

15 plicant.

1 mark for each question. Total: 15

Exercise 8.8

1 We prop.

2 You wipe.

3 They sup up.

4 You shake before.

5 They grow up.

6 He is in mourning.

7 We scorch.

8 You gnash your teeth.

9 I grind.

10 You fold.

11 You quiver.

12 You throttle.

13 We wipe our noses.

14 He nods to.

15 They quiver.

1 mark for each question. Total: 15

Exercise 8.9

1 To involve someone. **plico.**

2 Mournful. **lugeo.**

3 Growing up. **adolesco.**

4 A point of balance. **fulcio.**

5 Involved. **plico.**

6 Taking in liquid. **sorbeo.**

7 Very hot. **torreo.**

8 A cleaning liquid. **tergeo.**

9 Teeth used for chewing. **molo.**

10 Worried. **ango.**

2 marks for each question. Total: 20

Exercise 8.10

1 I am running.

2 Am I running?

3 We send.

4 Do we send?

5 They are laughing.

6 Are they laughing?

7 They are coming.

8 Are they coming?

9 He rules.

10 Does he rule?

11 Are you hurrying?

12 Are you listening?

13 Are they singing?

14 Is he sleeping?

15 Are you coming?

16 Are they running?

17 Are you afraid?

18 Is he coming?

19 Is he staying?

20 Are we working?

1 mark for each question. Total: 20

Exercise 8.11

1 Do you love the girl?

2 Are you looking at the woman?

3 Is the farmer working?

4 Are the farmers working?

5 Is he afraid of the goddess?

6 Are the sailors running?

7 Is the queen laughing?

8 Are the girls listening?

9 Do you have a spear?

10 Are we preparing dinner?

2 marks for each question. Total: 20

Exercise 8.12

1 Is Flavia a sailor?

2 Does the sailor have money?

3 Are the girls running?

4 Do the sailors love the girl?

5 Are you sending money?

6 Does Marcus love Flavia?

7 Do you love the girl, sailor?

8 Do the girls listen to the sailor?

9 Do the women praise the goddess?

10 Are the farmers holding spears?

3 marks for each question. Total: 30

Exercise 8.13

1 audisne?

2 dormiuntne?

3 clamone?

4 laboramusne?

5 laudatne?

6 sedemusne?

7 timetne?

8 curruntne?

9 ducimusne?

10 spectasne?

1 mark for each question. Total: 10

Exercise 8.14

1 puellane pugnat?

2 puellaene pugnant?

3 nautane currit?

4 nautaene currunt?

5 feminane venit?

6 puellaene dormiunt?

7 reginane ridet?

8 reginaene regunt?

9 cenane venit?

10 Flaviane audit?

2 marks for each question. Total: 20

Exercise 8.15

1 feminane cenam parat?

2 puellaene villas amant?

3 Marcusne Flaviam spectat?

4 hastaene nautas necant?

5 agricolaene reginam spectant?

6 Flaviane nauta est?

7 puellaene Romanae sunt?

8 nautaene reginam audiunt?

9 Marcusne cenam amat?

10 hastaene necant?

3 marks for each question. Total: 30

9

Marcus is blushing.(2) Why is Marcus blushing?(3) Marcus is blushing(2) because Flavia is kissing him.(4)

Flavia says to Marcus,'You are blushing, Marcus.(5) Why are you blushing?(2) Are you blushing because I am kissing you?'(4)

Marcus replies to Flavia:(3) 'Flavia, I am happy because you kiss me.(6) I am happy because you love me.(5) I am blushing because girls do not love me.(6) Why do you love me, Flavia?(4) Do you love me because I am a sailor?'(5)

Flavia replies to Marcus:(3) 'Marcus, I do not love you(3) because you are a sailor.(3) I love you because(3) you are handsome.(2) Do you love me, Marcus?'(3)

Marcus says, 'I love you, Flavia.'(5)

Flavia asks:(2) 'Why do you love me, Marcus?(4) Do you love me because(3) I prepare good dinners?'(3)

'I do not love you(3) because you prepare good dinners, Flavia,'(5) replies Marcus to Flavia.(3) I love you because(3) you are a beautiful girl.'(3)

Marcus kisses Flavia.(3) Flavia does not blush now.(4) Flavia kisses Marcus again.(4) Marcus does not blush now.(4) Marcus kisses Flavia again.(4) Marcus and Flavia are happy.(4)

Total: 125

Exercise 9.2

1 Flavia. (1)

2 A 2nd conjugation verb. (1)

3 cenas. (1)

4 sum. (1)

5 He replies/answers. Response. (2)

Total: 6

Exercise 9.3

1 Hearts = genitive; tarts = accusative.

2 Children = accusative; Mars Bar = ablative.

3 We = nominative; taxi = ablative.

4 Girl = vocative; room = ablative.

5 Favour = accusative; me = dative.

2 marks for each question. Total: 10

Exercise 9.4

1 Teacher = nominative; boy = accusative. (2)

2 Boy = vocative. (1)

3 Teacher = nominative; stick = ablative. (2)

4 Me = accusative; sir = vocative. (2)

5 Boy = dative; you = accusative; trouble = genitive. (3)

Total: 10

Exercise 9.5

1 Apple = accusative; teacher = dative.

2 Freddie = vocative; teacher = nominative.

3 Mum = nominative; me = dative.

4 You = dative; boy = nominative.

5 Freddie = vocative; teacher = nominative.

2 marks for each question. Total: 10

Exercise 9.6

1 agricolae

2 puellas

3 via

4 nautis

5 feminarum

6 vias

7 aquis

8 puellae

9 incolarum

10 agricolis

11 aquae

12 femina

13 dea!

14 ira

15 sagitta

16 pecuniae

17 ancillarum

18 puellis

19 puellae

20 terra

21 turbas

22 ancillae

23 poetae

24 cena

25 incolae

26 insulae

27 insularum

28 aqua

29 ira

30 sagittis

31 incolis

32 insulam

33 insulas

34 turbis

35 Flaviae

36 terrae

37 poetis

38 poetarum

39 undarum

40 turbae

1 mark for each question. Total: 40

Exercise 9.7

1 ira deae.

2 turba incolarum.

3 incolae viae.

4 cena agricolae.

5 pecunia poetae.

6 villa reginae.

7 filia feminae.

8 aqua insulae.

9 nautae patriae.

10 turbae puellarum.

2 marks for each question. Total: 20

Exercise 9.8

1 turbae incolarum.

2 sagittis nautae.

3 incolis terrae.

4 poetis patriae.

5 pecunia reginae.

6 hastis agricolarum.

7 feminis insularum.

8 reginae incolarum.

9 ira turbae.

10 incolis patriae.

2 marks for each question. Total: 20

Exercise 9.9

1 feminae — of the woman

2 agricolis — by/with/from the farmers

3 filiae — to/for the daughter

4 nautarum — of the sailors

5 puellis — to/for the girls

6 aquae — of the water

7 turbis — to/for the crowds

8 poetae — of the poet

9 undarum — of the waves

10 deae — of the goddess

11 villa — by/with/from the villa

12 hastis — by/with/from the spears

13 pecuniae — to/for money

14 incolae — inhabitants

15 irae	of anger
16 sagitta	by/with/from the arrow
17 regina	the queen
18 feminarum	of the women
19 cenae	dinners
20 deae	to/for the goddess

2 marks for each question. Total: 40

Exercise 9.10

1 The spear of the sailor.	(2)
2 The spear of the sailor kills.	(3)
3 The daughter of the queen.	(2)
4 The daughter of the queen is coming.	(3)
5 The maidservant of the poet.	(2)
6 The maidservant of the poet is singing.	(3)
7 The daughter of the woman.	(2)
8 The daughter of the woman is afraid.	(3)
9 The queen of the island.	(2)
10 The queen of the island is laughing.	(3)

Total: 25

Exercise 9.11

1 A crowd of sailors is coming.	(3)
2 The farmers frighten the girls.	(3)
3 The farmers frighten the girls with spears.	(4)
4 The daughter of the farmer is singing.	(3)
5 The daughters of the farmer are not singing.	(4)
6 The sailor loves the daughter of the queen.	(4)
7 The woman prepares the dinner of/for the farmer.	(4)
8 We are preparing dinner for the farmers.	(3)
9 The sailors kill the inhabitants with arrows.	(4)
10 We see a crowd of girls.	(3)

Total: 35

Exercise 9.12

1 aquam agricolae do.

2 aquam agricolis do.

3 pecuniam incolae ostendo.

4 pecuniam incolis ostendo.

5 hastas nautis damus.

3 marks for each question. Total: 15

Exercise 9.13

1 The girl gives money to the farmer. (4)

2 The girl gives money to the farmers. (4)

3 The poet shows the island to the sailor. (4)

4 The poet shows the island to the sailors. (4)

5 The woman gives water to the poet. (4)

6 The woman gives water to the poets. (4)

7 I give a spear to the farmer. (3)

8 We show the villa to the woman. (3)

9 You are preparing the dinner of/for the sailor. (3)

10 I am preparing arrows for the sailors. (3)

Total: 36

Exercise 9.14

1 turba puellarum. (2)

2 sagittae nautarum necant. (3)

3 poeta turbam agricolarum videt. (4)

4 filia agricolae cantat. (3)

5 ancillae cenam reginae parant. (4)

6 nauta agricolas hastis necat. (4)

Total: 20

Exercise 9.15

1 paro. (1)

2 cenam paro. (2)

3 cenam agricolae paro. (3)

4 damus. (1)

5 pecuniam damus. (2)

6 pecuniam puellis damus. (3)

7 ostendit. (1)

8 agricola ostendit. (2)

9 agricola hastas ostendit. (3)

10 hastas ostendit. (2)

Total: 20

Exercise 9.16

1 We sleep.

2 He sits.

3 I send.

4 You run.

5 You shout.

6 They lead.

7 He answers.

8 You put.

9 We hurry.

10 You come.

1 mark for each question. Total: 10

Exercise 9.17

1 The poets are afraid.

2 The queen is coming.

3 You hear the waves.

4 We have arrows.

5 The inhabitants sleep.

2 marks for each question. Total: 10

Exercise 9.18

1 The farmer loves the land.

2 Sailors do not fear waves.

3 The maidservants listen to the queen.

4 The crowd frightens the girls.

5 The poet takes the money.

3 marks for each question. Total: 15

Exercise 9.19

1 maneo.

2 venimus.

3 timet.

4 dormiunt.

5 respondent.

6 mittis.

7 clamo.

8 dicitis.

9 spectat.

10 ponimus.

1 mark for each question. Total: 10

Exercise 9.20

1 agricolae currunt.
2 insulam video.
3 turbas non amo.
4 reginam audimus.
5 regina dormit.

2 marks for each question. Total: 10

Exercise 9.21

1 nautae aquam amant.
2 ancilla cenam parat.
3 puella poetam audit.
4 femina turbam spectat.
5 regina terram regit.

3 marks for each question. Total: 15

Exercise 9.22

1 viae	roads
2 villae	villas
3 cenae	dinners
4 hastae	spears
5 deae	goddesses

2 marks for each question. Total: 10

Exercise 9.23

1 hasta	spear
2 femina	woman
3 regina	queen
4 agricola	farmer
5 puella	girl

2 marks for each question. Total: 10

Exercise 9.24

1 capit.	He takes.
2 facis.	You make.
3 curro.	I run.
4 respondet.	He answers.
5 rogas.	You ask.

2 marks for each question. Total: 10

Exercise 9.25

1	venimus.	We come.
2	dicitis.	You say.
3	mittunt.	They send.
4	vident.	They see.
5	amatis.	You love.

2 marks for each question. Total: 10

Exercise 9.26

1	puellae nautas vident.	The girls see the sailors.
2	nautae puellas amant.	The sailors see the girls.
3	feminae cenas parant.	The women prepare dinners.
4	agricolae reginas audiunt.	The farmers listen to the queens.
5	filiae hastas tenent.	The daughters are holding spears.

3+3 marks for each question. Total: 30

Exercise 9.27

1	agricola filiam amat.	The farmer loves his daughter.
2	puella hastam spectat.	The girl is looking at the spear.
3	femina deam audit.	The woman listens to the goddess.
4	nauta hastam mittit.	The sailor sends the spear.
5	femina filiam habet.	The woman has a daughter.

3+3 marks for each question. Total: 30

Exercise 10.1

Sextus and Flavia are pupils.[4] They are working in school.[3] They are writing.[1] Sextus does not like Flavia.[3] He does not like Flavia[3] because she is a girl.[3] He does not like girls.[3] Flavia does not like Sextus.[3] She does not like Sextus[2] because he is a boy.[3] Flavia does not like boys,[3] except for Marcus.[2]

Suddenly Sextus thumps Flavia.[4] Sextus often thumps girls.[4] Flavia therefore thumps Sextus.[4] Sextus thumps Flavia again.[4] They fight.[1] The teacher sees Sextus and Flavia.[4] 'What are you doing?' he shouts.[3] 'Why are you fighting?'[2] Sextus and Flavia don't fight now.[5] They look at the teacher.[2] 'Sextus always thumps me,' answers Flavia.[6] 'Flavia always thumps me,' answers Sextus.[6] The teacher is angry.[3] He punishes Sextus.[2] Sextus cries.[2] The teacher also punishes Flavia.[4] Flavia also cries.[3] Flavia and Sextus are not happy.[5] They do not like the teacher.[3]

Total: 100

Exercise 10.2

1 Plural. (1)

2 3rd. (1)

3 Accusative. (1)

4 Accusative. Object of the verb. (2)

Total: 5

Exercise 10.3

1 The friend is running.

2 I have a friend.

3 The friends are fighting.

4 You do not have friends.

5 We have swords.

6 They fear the master.

7 The messenger is coming.

8 The messengers are coming.

9 The slave is hurrying.

10 You are looking at the walls.

2 marks for each question. Total: 20

Exercise 10.4

1 He has a horse.

2 We love horses.

3 The slaves are fighting.

4 You have a son.

5 The god is shouting.

6 They fear the master.

7 The messenger is coming.

8 The messengers are coming.

9 The slave is hurrying.

10 You watch the walls.

2 marks for each question. Total: 20

Exercise 10.5

1 The master has a slave.
2 The masters have slaves.
3 The allies love horses.
4 The slaves are preparing food.
5 The slaves listen to the master.

6 The sword frightens the friend.
7 The god is not afraid of swords.
8 The friends are afraid of the wind.
9 The master sends a messenger.
10 The swords kill the slaves.

3 marks for each question. Total: 30

Exercise 10.6

1 The allies have swords.
2 The god calls the master.
3 The master fears the god.
4 The son listens to the master.
5 The slave is carrying food.

6 The horses love food.
7 Slaves do not have friends.
8 The master likes the place.
9 The allies are looking at the walls.
10 The friends are looking at the wall.

3 marks for each question. Total: 30

Exercise 10.7

1 servus festinat.
2 servi festinant.
3 dominus venit.
4 domini veniunt.
5 equi currunt.

6 amicus clamat.
7 amici pugnant.
8 equus dormit.
9 filius timet.
10 deus non timet.

2 marks for each question. Total: 20

Exercise 10.8

1 gladium habeo.
2 gladios habeo.
3 murum videmus.
4 muros videmus.
5 equos amant.

6 nuntium auditis.
7 dominum timemus.
8 cibum paras.
9 equos videt.
10 servum laudant.

2 marks for each question. Total: 20

Exercise 10.9

1 nuntius filium habet.
2 filius gladium habet.
3 filius gladios amat.

4 venti equos terrent.
5 dominus cibum amat.

3 marks for each question. Total: 15

Chapter 10

Exercise 10.10

1 deus dominum terret.

2 dei locum amant.

3 gladius equum necat.

4 dominus filium habet.

5 servi equos ducunt.

3 marks for each question. Total: 15

Exercise 10.11

1 Flick = ablative

Wrist = genitive

Batsman = nominative

Ball = accusative (4)

2 Bat = ablative (1)

3 Ball = genitive (1)

4 Ground = ablative (1)

5 He = nominative

Ball = accusative

Umpire = vocative (3)

Total: 10

Exercise 10.12

One mark is given for each noun, and one for correctly stating which case it should be in.

Total: 10

Exercise 10.13

1 servi

2 gladio

3 gladiis

4 muris

5 equum

6 amici

7 cibo

8 nuntio

9 murorum

10 filio

11 nuntios

12 amicis

13 equis

14 domine!

15 cibi

16 servi!

17 equo

18 filium

19 muro

20 equorum

1 mark for each question. Total: 20

Exercise 11.1

Flavia has a friend.(3) Flavia's friend is Marcus.(4) Marcus has a girlfriend.(3) Marcus's girlfriend is Flavia.(4)

Marcus is walking along the road.(3) Flavia is also walking along the road.(4) She is hurrying to school.(3) She is crying.(1) She is crying because(2) Sextus is always thumping her in school.(5) She does not like Sextus because(4) he is a wicked boy.(3)

Marcus sees Flavia.(3) Marcus immediately asks, 'Flavia,(4) why are you crying?'(2) Flavia replies to Marcus:(3) 'Oh Marcus, I'm crying because(3) Sextus thumps me in school.(4) Then the teacher punishes me.(4) He is a wicked man.(3) He never punishes Sextus.(3) I don't like Sextus.(3) He is a wicked boy.'(3)

Marcus is angry(3) because Flavia is crying.(3) He kisses Flavia.(2) Flavia is now happy(4) because Marcus kisses her.(4) She laughs.(1) Marcus and Flavia walk to school.(5) Marcus and Flavia are happy.(4)

Total: 100

Exercise 11.2

1 Flavia (lines 1/2/4/8/9/14/15/16/17); Flaviae (line 1); Flaviam (lines 8/14); amicam (line 2); amica (line 2); viam (lines 4/5). (1)

2 Genitive. (1)

3 3rd. (1)

4 Plural. (1)

5 Friend. Amicable. (2)

Total: 6

Exercise 11.3

1 servus aquam amat.

2 servi cenam parant.

3 nautae cibum laudant.

4 agricolae equos amant.

5 Graeci Romanos necant.

6 agricola equum non habet.

7 nuntius virum spectat.

8 gladium et hastam habeo.

9 sagittae equos terrent.

10 domini villas habent.

3 marks for each question. Total: 30

Exercise 11.4

1 servus agricolae currit. (3)

2 servi terram hastis delent. (4)

3 agricola pecuniam servis dat. (4)

4 ventus villam domini delet. (4)

5 incolas gladiis terremus. (3)

6 femina pecuniam amicis dat. (4)

7 turba servorum venit. (3)

8 villam amico ostendo. (3)

9 deam insulae laudant. (3)

10 agricola murum gladio delet. (4)

Total: 35

Exercise 11.5

1 in equis

2 in muro

3 in villa

4 in villam

5 trans insulam

6 cum amico

7 cum nautis

8 prope aquam

9 a muro

10 in via

2 marks for each question. Total: 20

Exercise 11.6

1 ad aquam

2 prope locum

3 per viam

4 ex aqua

5 a nuntiis

6 in viis

7 ad murum

8 per aquam

9 contra socios

10 trans viam

2 marks for each question. Total: 20

Exercise 11.7

1 ad puellam

2 servo

3 amicis

4 ad insulam

5 ad aquam

6 puero

7 ad murum

8 nautis

9 ad amicum

10 Romanis

2 marks for each question. Total: 20

Exercise 11.8

1 cum amicis

2 cum puella

3 cum gladiis/gladiis

4 cum servo

5 ira

6 sagittis

7 cum equis

8 cum ancilla

9 gladio

10 cum Romanis

2 marks for each question. Total: 20

Exercise 11.9

1 cum amicis

2 in equo

3 contra incolas

4 cum Sexto

5 prope viam

6 contra dominum

7 in murum

8 in turba

9 cum servis

10 cum cibo

2 marks for each question. Total: 20

Exercise 11.10

1 with Marcus

2 out of the water

3 in the road

4 into the road

5 down from the wall

6 along the road

7 along the roads

8 against the Romans

9 to the island

10 to the islands

2 marks for each question. Total: 20

Exercise 11.11

1 on land

2 across the road

3 away from the islands

4 with the allies

5 near the place

6 on the wall

7 against the wind

8 on horses

9 with a friend

10 in the crowd

2 marks for each question. Total: 20

Exercise 11.12

1 near the island

2 with sailors

3 into the wall

4 with women

5 against the farmers

6 in water

7 against Sextus

8 across the water

9 to the villa

10 away from the messenger

2 marks for each question. Total: 20

Exercise 11.13

1 I am sitting on the wall.

2 We are walking to the villa.

3 He is fighting against the Romans.

4 We are running along the road.

5 You live in a villa.

6 We live near an island.

7 He is walking across the road.

8 We are singing with friends.

9 You are running away from the villa.

10 You are running into the villa.

3 marks for each question. Total: 30

Exercise 11.14

1 in via curro.

2 in viam curro.

3 ab insula venimus.

4 in loco manent.

5 in muro sedet.

6 in villa dormiunt.

7 contra Graecos pugno.

8 trans viam festinas.

9 cum amico cantat.

10 ad murum ambulant.

3 marks for each question. Total: 30

Exercise 11.15

1 in muro

2 in murum

3 in via

4 in viam

5 in villas

6 in villis

7 in locum

8 in loco

9 in turba

10 in aquam

2 marks for each question. Total: 20

Exercise 11.16

1 The boy is running away from the teacher. (4)

2 The girl comes with her friends. (4)

3 The sailors are sitting on the wall. (4)

4 The slave lives in a villa. (4)

5 Slaves live in villas. (4)

6 The man hurries along the roads. (4)

7 The horse is walking towards the wall. (4)

8 The Romans are fighting against the Greeks. (4)

9 He rules in the country. (3)

10 A crowd of girls is running into the road. (5)

Total: 40

Exercise 11.17

1 The boy sees a friend in the street. (5)

2 The girls are sitting on horses. (4)

3 Marcus and Flavia are walking along the street. (6)

4 The slave is carrying water into the villa. (4)

5 The maidservant is preparing dinner in the villa. (5)

6 The slave is leading the horse out of the water. (4)

7 The farmers are fighting against the sailors. (4)

8 The sailors are running away from the island. (4)

9 The boys are working near the teacher. (4)

10 The farmer sends a messenger to the friend. (5)

Total: 45

Exercise 11.18

1 servi in villam currunt.

2 socii contra amicos pugnant.

3 puella in equo sedet.

4 turba per viam festinat.

5 turbae per vias festinant.

4 marks for each question. Total: 20

Exercise 11.19

1 magister in insula scribit. (4)

2 servi cibum trans viam portant. (5)

3 vir pecuniam prope locum ponit. (5)

4 dominus servum ad locum mittit. (5)

5 magistri ancillas e villa mittunt. (5)

Total: 24

Exercise 11.20

1	punimus.	We punish.
2	dant.	They give.
3	dico.	I say.
4	audit.	He hears.
5	ducis.	You lead.
6	delent.	They destroy.
7	mittit.	He sends.
8	flent.	They cry.
9	sedetis.	You sit.
10	scribit.	He writes.

2 marks for each question. Total: 20

Exercise 11.21

1	We destroy.	1st person plural.
2	You put.	2nd person singular.
3	They punish.	3rd person plural.
4	You do.	2nd person plural.
5	You write.	2nd person singular.
6	I come.	1st person singular.
7	He cries.	3rd person singular.
8	We sleep.	1st person plural.
9	We give.	1st person plural.
10	You show.	2nd person plural.

3 marks for each question. Total: 30

Exercise 12.1

Flavia is walking to school with Marcus.(6) Flavia likes Marcus.(3) He is a good friend.(3) Flavia does not like Sextus.(4) He is a wicked boy.(3) They are now approaching school.(4) Many pupils are playing near school.(5) Marcus does not see Sextus.(4) He enters the school.(2)

Boys are working there.(3) They are reading books(2) and writing.(2) The teacher however is not present in school.(5) Marcus looks at the boys.(3) He sees Sextus.(2) He laughs.(1) He runs towards Sextus.(3) He thumps Sextus.(2) He thumps Sextus again and again.(4) 'Stop!' shouts Sextus.(3) 'Why are you thumping me?'(3) Marcus stops.(3) 'I am thumping you because(3) you are always thumping Flavia,'(3) replies Marcus.(2) 'Flavia is my girlfriend.(3) You are a wicked boy, Sextus!'(5) Marcus thumps Sextus again,(4) then departs.(2) Sextus is not happy.(3) He is crying.(1) Marcus is a wicked boy.(4)

Total: 100

Exercise 12.2

1 cum Marco (line 1); in ludo (line 8).

2 ad ludum (lines 1/3–4); prope ludum (lines 4–5); ad Sextum (lines 9–10).

3 Masculine.

4 Accusative.

5 sum.

1 mark for each question. Total: 5

Exercise 12.3

1 The boy and the man are running in the field. (6)

2 The boy and the man are running into the field. (6)

3 The teacher is writing a book. (3)

4 The teacher is writing a book for the boys. (4)

5 The girl does not love the boy. (4)

6 The boy's books are in the villa. (5)

7 The boys give a book to the teacher. (4)

8 We see horses in the fields. (4)

9 A crowd of boys is hurrying towards the field. (5)

10 The man does not read books. (4)

Total: 45

Exercise 12.4

1 I love you. (3)

2 Do you love me? (3)

3 He loves me. (2)

4 We love you. (2)

5 They love us. (2)

6 We are running, you are wallking. (4)

7 I am laughing, you are crying. (4)

8 You are departing, we are staying. (4)

9 The girls are looking at us. (3)

10 You are Roman boys, we are Greek boys. (8)

Total: 35

Exercise 12.5

1 I am a girl, you are a boy. (6)

2 I love you, but you do not love me. (8)

3 We are Romans, you are Greeks. (6)

4 The teacher asks: 'What are you doing, boys? I am working.' (8)

5 The boys reply: 'We are playing, teacher.' (5)

6 The teacher shouts: 'I therefore do not like you.' (7)

7 The boys shout: 'Why do you not like us, teacher?' (7)

8 The teacher replies: 'I do not like you because you are not working.' (8)

9 The boys shout: 'Teacher, we are not listening to you. We do not like you.' (9)

10 The teacher replies: 'Boys, you do not like me, I do not like you.' (11)

Total: 75

Exercise 12.6

1 ego Marcus sum, tu Sextus es. (6)

2 me amant. (2)

3 te amamus. (3)

4 magister nos non amat. (4)

5 magistrum non amamus. (4)

6 vos specto. (3)

7 te moneo. (3)

8 magister/dominus me terret. (3)

9 servi nos spectant. (3)

10 vos timemus, nautae. (4)

Total: 35

Exercise 12.7

1 belli

2 verba

3 periculo

4 scuta

5 oppido

6 templorum

7 verbis

8 auxilio

9 pericula

10 proelii

11 vino

12 auro

13 caelo

14 proeliorum

15 scuti

16 scuto

17 periculis

18 bello

19 oppida

20 verbis

1 mark for each question. Total: 20

Exercise 12.8

1 Boys love wars. (3)

2 I am looking at the temples. (2)

3 The slave is carrying a shield. (3)

4 The slaves are carrying shields. (3)

5 Women love gold. (3)

6 The farmer is looking at the sky. (3)

7 Sailors do not fear dangers. (4)

8 The sailor likes wine. (3)

9 Help is not coming. (3)

10 Farmers love battles. (3)

Total: 30

Exercise 12.9

1 The girl fears the war. (3)

2 The master gives help to the slaves. (4)

3 The temple is in the town. (4)

4 The boys do not listen to the teacher's words. (5)

5 Girls do not play in temples. (5)

6 The queen has a sword. (3)

7 The teacher frightens the girls with words. (4)

8 Sailors often fight in battles. (5)

9 The Romans capture the town. (3)

10 They capture the town with the help of the Greeks. (4)

Total: 40

Exercise 12.10

1 agricolae bellum parant. (3)

2 feminae bella non amant. (4)

3 puella aurum amat. (3)

4 verba audimus. (2)

5 servus vinum portat. (3)

6 caelum specto. (2)

7 oppidum amamus. (2)

8 vir periculum videt. (3)

9 socii scuta habent. (3)

10 nauta proelia et bella timet. (5)

Total: 30

Exercise 12.11

1 in oppido habitamus. (3)

2 aurum in templum portamus. (4)

3 puellae e periculo currunt. (4)

4 Graeci contra Romanos pugnant. (4)

5 servus vinum domini amat. (4)

6 nuntii in templo dormiunt. (4)

7 scuta Romanorum puellas terrent. (4)

8 nautae templa oppidi spectant. (4)

9 periculum in proelio video. (4)

10 servi amicos in bello necant. (5)

Total: 40

Exercise 12.12

1 nautae   3 agris

2 servi   4 vino

5 amice

6 templa

7 dominorum

8 gladio

9 pecuniae

10 bella

11 pueris

12 viarum

13 hastae

14 muris

15 equi

16 oppida

17 periculo

18 cibo

19 cibum

20 hastas

1 mark for each question. Total: 20

Exercise 12.13

1 via

2 muri

3 puellarum

4 periculi

5 periculorum

6 gladio

7 oppidis

8 equo

9 O, puella!

10 amico

11 cibo

12 muri

13 puero

14 hastis

15 templa

16 bellis

17 dominorum/magistrorum

18 periculo

19 puellae

20 pecuniae

1 mark for each question. Total: 20

Exercise 12.14

1 of the road/to the road/for the road; roads

2 of the spears

3 of the wall/walls

4 to/for/by/with/from food

5 to/for/by/with/from words

6 towns

7 to/for/by/with/from swords

8 of friends

9 to/for/by/with/from wine

10 of the field/fields

11 to/for/by/with/from slaves

12 of/to/for the sailor; sailors

13 to/for/by/with/from boys

14 wars

15 temple

16 to/for/by/with/from the friend

17 to/for/by/with/from towns

18 of wine

19 of fields

20 to/for/by/with/from the horse

1 mark for each question. Total: 20

Exercise 13.1

Marcus and Flavia are in town.[5] They enter a pub.[2] When they enter the pub,[3] they sit.[1] They eat food[2] and drink wine.[3] They stay in the pub for a long time.[3] The food is good.[3] Flavia likes the food.[3] The wine is good.[3] Marcus and Flavia are happy.[4]

Four sailors are also present in the pub.[5] They are standing near Marcus and Flavia.[4] Because the wine is good,[3] the sailors drink a lot.[3] Soon therefore they are drunk.[4] Flavia looks at the drunken sailors.[4] She fears the sailors.[2] And so she says to Marcus, 'Marcus,[4] the sailors are drunk.[3] I am frightened.[2] I want to depart.'[2] Marcus looks at the sailors.[3] When he sees them,[3] he is angry.[2] Marcus and Flavia walk out of the pub.[4] The four sailors also walk out of the pub.[5]

Total: 85

Exercise 13.2

1 Ablative. After the preposition **in**. (2)

2 Neuter. (1)

3 Subject: **Flavia**. Object: **cibum**. (2)

Total: 5

Exercise 13.3

1 the good boy

2 the good girl

3 good wine

4 happy slaves

5 many women

6 the big temple

7 the big temples

8 the angry farmer

9 the small villa

10 great danger

11 many dangers

12 a good sword

13 good swords

14 the tired horse

15 big walls

16 wicked words

17 frightened friends

18 the tired slave

19 the savage master

20 the angry goddess

21 tired horses

22 savage wars

23 many spears

24 the savage teacher

25 the big wall

26 the good man

27 angry slaves

28 the small temple

29 the big island

30 the angry sailor

2 marks for each question. Total: 60

Exercise 13.4

1 puella parva

2 puellae parvae

3 servus fessus

4 servi fessi

5 bellum magnum

6 bella magna

7 servus laetus

8 multa pecunia

9 scuta magna

10 dominus/magister iratus

11 verbum bonum

12 cibus malus

13 venti saevi

14 proelia magna

15 bellum saevum

16 dea irata

17 multa pericula

18 vir bonus

19 cibus bonus

20 turba magna

21 liber bonus

22 multis servis

23 dominorum/magistrorum iratorum

24 puellae bonae

25 amici fessi

26 multas hastas

27 vinum bonum

28 servis laetis

29 verbis bonis

30 templo parvo

2 marks for each question. Total: 60

Exercise 13.5

1 The slave is preparing good food. (4)

2 The boy is looking at many girls. (4)

3 The angry teacher warns the wicked boys. (5)

4 The girls are Roman. (3)

5 The farmer has many fields. (4)

6 There are many horses in the fields. (5)

7 Many boys are running along the road. (5)

8 The tired sailors are sleeping in the villa. (5)

9 The wicked girls are listening to the good teacher. (5)

10 The good boys fear the savage war. (5)

Total: 45

Exercise 13.6

1 The master gives much money to the slaves. (5)
2 The master gives money to many slaves. (5)
3 I often read good books. (4)
4 The teacher is writing a big book. (4)
5 The boys are happy because the teacher is good. (7)
6 The tired boys are playing in the big fields. (6)
7 The Romans capture many towns. (4)
8 Many friends praise the good food. (5)
9 The boy frightens the girl with the big shield. (5)
10 The happy boy has a big spear. (5)

Total: 50

Exercise 13.7

1 The Romans have many swords and many arrows. (7)
2 We do not listen to the words of the angry teacher. (5)
3 We do not listen to the angry words of the teacher. (5)
4 The master gives wine to the tired slaves. (5)
5 The happy slaves drink wine in the big town. (7)
6 The words of the angry girls frighten the boys. (5)
7 Good boys read many books. (5)
8 The master is angry because the boys are not good. (8)
9 The master gives many spears to his good friends. (6)
10 The boys are playing in the fields with their good friends. (7)

Total: 60

Exercise 13.8

1 The teacher gives gold to the good boys. (5)
2 The good woman gives water to the tired sailor. (6)
3 The slaves prepare food for the good boys. (5)
4 The girl does not like the savage sailor. (4)
5 Farmers do not like big towns. (4)
6 They hear the words of the angry teacher. (4)
7 The crowd of angry women hurries into the town. (6)

8 The frightened girl is sitting in the big villa. (6)

9 The angry sailor frightens the girl. (4)

10 The girl fears the angry sailor. (4)

Total: 48

Exercise 13.9

1 magister laetus est quod pueri boni sunt. (7)

2 puellae bonae nautas timent. (4)

3 puellae perterritae per viam currunt. (5)

4 multi viri templum magnum spectant. (5)

5 puer magistrum/dominum iratum timet. (4)

Total: 25

Exercise 13.10

1 multi viri pericula belli timent.

2 femina perterrita e templo currit.

3 quod pueri currunt, fessi sunt.

4 multi servi hastas magnas habent.

5 dominus aquam servo fesso dat.

5 marks for each question. Total: 25

Exercise 13.11

1 insulae	islands
2 pueri	boys
3 agri	fields
4 pericula	dangers
5 verba	words

2 marks for each question. Total: 10

Exercise 13.12

1 turba	crowd
2 discipulus	pupil
3 liber	book
4 scutum	shield
5 vinum	wine

2 marks for each question. Total: 10

Exercise 13.13

1	legimus.	We read.
2	adsunt.	They are present.
3	discedunt.	They depart.
4	deletis.	You destroy.
5	scribunt.	They write.

2 marks for each question. Total: 10

Exercise 13.14

1	do.	I give.
2	ostendit.	He shows.
3	fles.	You weep.
4	scribo.	I write.
5	discedis.	You depart.

2 marks for each question. Total: 10

Exercise 13.15

1	pueri in agris ludunt.	The boys are playing in the fields.	(3+4)
2	discipuli libros legunt.	Pupils read books.	(3+3)
3	viri bella timent.	Men fear wars.	(3+3)
4	servi scuta habent.	The slaves have shields.	(3+3)
5	amici in proeliis pugnant.	The friends are fighting in battles.	(3+4)

Total: 32

Exercise 13.16

1	puella vinum amat.	The girl likes wine.	(3+3)
2	periculum nautam terret.	The danger frightens the sailor.	(3+3)
3	servus in villa laborat.	The slave is working in the villa.	(3+4)
4	nuntius equum ducit.	The messenger is leading a horse.	(3+3)
5	puer contra puellam pugnat.	The boy is fighting against the girl.	(3+4)

Total: 32

Exercise 14.1

Marcus and Flavia walk out of the pub[5] because Flavia is afraid of the four drunk sailors.[6] The sailors also walk out of the pub.[4] 'Hurry, Marcus![2] I am afraid of them,'[2] shouts Flavia.[2] They decide to hurry.[2] The sailors also hurry along the road now.[5] 'Run, Marcus!' shouts Flavia.[3] They run.[1] The sailors also run.[3] In this way the sailors soon catch up with Marcus and Flavia.[6]

The first sailor shouts:[3] 'What are you doing here?[3] Answer!'[1]

Marcus answers[2] 'We are walking home.'[2]

The second sailor asks[3] 'Who is the girl?'[3]

Marcus answers angrily[3] 'The girl is Flavia.[3] She is my girlfriend.'[3]

The third sailor shouts[3] 'Your girlfriend?[2] Flavia is beautiful.[3] Do you love me, Flavia?'[4]

The four sailors laugh.[3]

'Where is the money?'[3] shouts the fourth sailor.[3]

Marcus is now very angry.[4] 'We don't have money.[3] Push off!'[1]

The four sailors now depart.[4]

Total: 100

Exercise 14.2

1 A preposition. (1)

2 Plural. (1)

3 2nd. (2)

4 rideo. (1)

5 She shouts. Clamour. (1)

Total: 6

Exercise 14.3

1 festina!

2 ride!

3 scribe!

4 cape!

5 dormi!

6 audi!

7 bibe!

8 mitte!

9 dele!

10 canta!

1 mark for each question. Total: 10

Exercise 14.4

1 laborate!

2 manete!

3 currite!

4 venite!

5 legite!

6 ludite!

7 consumite!

8 videte!

9 este!

10 ambulate!

1 mark for each question. Total: 10

Exercise 14.5

1 Laugh, boy! (2)

2 Run, slaves! (2)

3 Listen to the teacher, boys! (3)

4 Come, friend! (2)

5 Take the town, slaves! (3)

6 Look at the temple, slaves! (3)

7 Prepare the food, slave! (3)

8 Boys, work! (2)

9 Stay here, Marcus! (3)

10 Punish the slave, master! (3)

11 Give money to the boy, girl! (4)

12 Fight, sailors! (2)

13 Kill the Greeks, Romans! (3)

14 Send gold to the master! (4)

15 Prepare dinner, woman! (3)

16 Read the book, poet! (3)

17 Friend, give food to the slaves! (4)

18 Listen to my words, master! (4)

19 Kill the Romans! (2)

20 Come to the big town, friends! (5)

Total: 60

Exercise 14.6

1 Take the money, slave! (3)

2 Come to the town, friend! (4)

3 Drink the wine! (2)

4 Work, boys! (2)

5 Work, friend! (2)

6 Give money to the boys! (3)

7 Rule the land, queen! (3)

8 Fight, boy! (2)

9 Watch! (1)

10 Sing, girls! (2)

11 Fight against the Romans! (3)

12 Look at the temples, sailors! (3)

13 Drink the wine, queen! (3)

14 Capture the town! (2)

15 Send help! (2)

16 Sleep, girls! (2)

17 Run, slaves! (2)

18 Send the gold, queen! (3)

19 Move the shields, slaves! (3)

20 Kill the slaves, Romans! (3)

Total: 50

Exercise 14.7

1 We are drinking wine.

2 They are looking at the temples.

3 I fear danger.

4 They are reading the book.

5 He punishes the pupils.

2 marks for each question. Total: 10

Exercise 14.8

1 auxilium venit.

2 aurum amamus.

3 cibum consumunt.

4 templa deletis.

5 libros scribit.

2 marks for each question. Total: 10

Exercise 14.9

1 The pupils are happy.

2 The book is big.

3 We are good boys.

4 The woman is frightened.

5 The teachers are angry.

3 marks for each question. Total: 15

Exercise 14.10

1 equi fessi sunt.

2 puer bonus sum.

3 domini/magistri mali sunt.

4 templa magna sunt.

5 agricola laetus est.

3 marks for each question. Total: 15

Exercise 14.11

1 The slaves are working in the fields.

2 The girl does not love you.

3 The boy has many friends.

4 Wars do not frighten me.

5 I am not playing with my friends.

4 marks for each question. Total: 20

Exercise 14.12

1 magister nos non amat. (4)

2 semper iratus est. (3)

3 in via saepe ludimus. (4)

4 nos Romani sumus, sed vos Graeci estis. (7)

5 Graeci Romanos non amant. (4)

Total: 22

Exercise 14.13

1 agricola aquam habet.

2 ancilla hastam portat.

3 turba agricolam necat.

4 puella deam laudat.

5 filia reginam amat.

6 femina insulam videt.

7 poeta puellam amat.

8 sagitta poetam terret.

9 hasta nautam necat.

10 nauta feminas spectat.

3 marks for each question. Total: 30

Exercise 15.1

Marcus and Flavia and the four sailors are standing in the street.(6) Marcus is very angry.(4) He orders the sailors to depart.(3) Because the sailors are not afraid of Marcus, they laugh.(5) They shout to Marcus and Flavia:(3) 'Give us your money.(4) We want to buy wine.'(3) Marcus decides to frighten the sailors.(4) He has a new sword.(3) The sword is good and strong.(4) Marcus takes his sword(4) and immediately runs towards the sailors.(4) He shouts.(1) Flavia is frightened.(3) Marcus fights with the sailors.(4) He fights bravely.(2) He fights well.(2) The sailors however do not have swords.(4) And so Marcus soon overcomes the sailors.(5) The sailors flee.(2) Marcus looks at Flavia.(3) 'Our money is safe.(4) We are safe,' he says.(4) 'I love you, Marcus,' Flavia answers.(4)

Total: 85

Exercise 15.2

1 (i) date (line 4).

 (ii) quattuor (line 1)

 (iii) iratus (line 2); **vestram** (line 5); **novum** (line 7); **bonus** (line 7); **validus** (line 8); **suum** (line 8); **perterrita** (line 9); **nostra** (line 14); **tuta** (line 14); **tuti** (line 14).

 (iv) **vinum** (line 5). (4)

2 1st. (1)

Total: 5

Exercise 15.3

1 We want to play. (2)

2 We do not want to work. (3)

3 I want to hurry. (2)

4 The girls are preparing to sing. (3)

5 Marcus wants to fight. (3)

6 The sailors want to drink. (3)

7 The boy does not want to write. (4)

8 The pupils want to sleep. (3)

9 The poet wants to read a book. (4)

10 Masters always want to punish slaves. (5)

Total: 32

Exercise 15.4

1 He decides to stay. (2)

2 They are preparing to depart. (2)

3 The pupils decide to work. (3)

4 The slave decides to run. (3)

5 The teacher decides to punish the pupils. (4)

6 The sailors decide to take the money. (4)

7 The queen decides to rule the land. (4)

8 The Romans prepare to overcome the Greeks. (4)

9 The poet decides to write a book. (4)

10 The maidservants decide to prepare dinner. (4)

Total: 34

Exercise 15.5

1 The master orders the slaves to work. (4)

2 The teacher orders the pupils to write. (4)

3 Marcus orders the sailor to depart. (4)

4 Masters never order slaves to play. (5)

5 He orders the farmers to fight well. (4)

6 I order you to stay here. (5)

7 The queen orders the men to prepare the spears. (5)

8 The master orders the slave to lead the horse out of the field. (7)

9 The goddess orders the maidservants to look at the temple. (5)

10 The master orders the slaves to carry the water into the villa. (7)

Total: 50

Exercise 15.6

1 cantare.

2 videre.

3 ponere.

4 venire.

5 iubere.

6 constituere.

7 festinare.

8 ludere.

9 scribere.

10 esse.

1 mark for each question. Total: 10

Exercise 15.7

1 spectare.

2 legere.

3 manere.

4 pugnare.

5 mittere.

6 punire.

7 dare.

8 currere.

9 clamare.

10 ridere.

1 mark for each question. Total: 10

Exercise 15.8

1 ludere cupimus.

2 laborare constituunt.

3 bibere cupio.

4 pugnare constituitis.

5 cantare cupiunt.

2 marks for each question. Total: 10

Exercise 15.9

1 dominus/magister festinare constituit. (3)

2 regina insulam regere cupit. (4)

3 ancillae cenam parare constituunt. (4)

4 discipuli libros legere non cupiunt. (5)

5 nauta servum punire constituit. (4)

Total: 20

Exercise 15.10

1 domini servos laborare iubent.

2 me manere saepe iubes.

3 regina servum cantare iubet.

4 Flavia Marcum pugnare iubet.

5 domini/magistri pueros laborare iubent.

4 marks for each question. Total: 20

Exercise 15.11

1 vir servum pecuniam capere iubet. (5)

2 femina filiam trans viam ambulare iubet. (6)

3 regina servos cibum parare iubet. (5)

4 Marcus agricolam equum necare iubet. (5)

5 regina virum nuntium ad insulam mittere iubet. (7)

Total: 28

Exercise 15.12

1 We are sitting in the sacred temple. (4)

2 Marcus is a well known and famous sailor. (6)

3 Flavia is miserable because the sailors are wicked. (7)

4 The slaves are building a wall. (3)

5 The Romans are attacking the walls. (3)

6 The sailors are sailing towards the island. (4)

7 The farmers are throwing many spears. (4)

8 Attack the town, sailors! (3)

9 The wicked men attack the sacred town with spears and swords. (8)

10 The queen sails to the land and builds a new town. (8)

Total: 50

Exercise 15.13

1 femina aquam habet.

2 nauta hastam portat.

3 turba deam laudat.

4 dea filiam laudat.

5 regina nautam amat.

6 femina insulam spectat.

7 puella poetam amat.

8 sagittae agricolas terrent.

9 hasta feminam necat.

10 femina nautam spectat.

3 marks for each question. Total: 30

Exercise 16.1

Marcus and Flavia were safe.(4) Flavia was not frightened now.(4) She was even praising Marcus.(3) 'Marcus,(1) you are a brave and strong man.(5) I am happy because we are safe.(5) The sailors were afraid of you.(3) Even I was afraid of you.(4) Because the sailors were afraid of you,(4) they did not want to fight.(3)

Marcus said to Flavia(3) 'Flavia,(1) I am also happy(3) because we are safe.'(3)

'Marcus, come to my villa.(4) I have food.(2) I will prepare a good dinner.(3) You are my hero.'(3)

'Great!' shouted Marcus.(3)

Marcus was happy.(3) He liked food.(2) He also liked Flavia's dinners.(4) Marcus and Flavia therefore hurried to Flavia's villa.(5)

Total: 75

Exercise 16.2

1 pugnare (line 6). (1)

2 veni (line 9). (1)

3 Accusative. After the preposition ad. (2)

4 Singular. (1)

5 (i) 2nd.

  (ii) Singular.

  (iii) sum. (3)

6 Sailors. Nautical. (2)

Total: 10

Exercise 16.3

1 We were calling.

2 He was praising.

3 I was putting.

4 They were playing.

5 He was sending.

6 He was departing.

7 He was taking.

8 They were wanting.

9 He was.

10 I was doing.

11 He was playing.

12 We were walking.

13 You were praising.

14 He was running.

15 They were punishing.

16 He was moving.

17 You were coming.

18 They were.

19 We were seeing.

20 They were drinking.

21 He was walking.

22 I was sleeping.

23 He was coming.

24 You were laughing.

25 They were doing.

26 You were hearing.

27 We were taking.

28 He was carrying.

29 They were watching.

30 We were fighting.

1 mark for each question. Total: 30

Exercise 16.4

1 laudabat.

2 laborabamus.

3 stabam.

4 rogabat.

5 oppugnabant.

6 vocabamus.

7 aedificabas.

8 navigabatis.

9 spectabant.

10 necabat.

1 mark for each question. Total: 10

Exercise 16.5

1 videbas.

2 iubebamus.

3 monebant.

4 terrebam.

5 respondebat.

6 manebam.

7 ridebat.

8 timebant.

9 tenebatis.

10 habebamus.

1 mark for each question. Total: 10

Exercise 16.6

1 ducebat.

2 bibebant.

3 legebam.

4 mittebamus.

5 ludebat.

6 dicebat.

7 constituebant.

8 ponebatis.

9 discedebamus.

10 currebant.

1 mark for each question. Total: 10

Exercise 16.7

1 audiebant.

2 dormiebam.

3 veniebat.

4 iaciebamus.

5 audiebatis.

6 capiebamus.

7 faciebas.

8 veniebant.

9 dormiebat.

10 capiebas.

1 mark for each question. Total: 10

Exercise 16.8

1 monebant.

2 bibebat.

3 portabatis.

4 ridebamus.

5 cantabant.

6 spectabamus.

7 manebant.

8 mittebat.

9 currebas.

10 audiebant.

1 mark for each question. Total: 10

Exercise 16.9

1 Today I am walking; yesterday I was not walking. (5)

2 He is working now; yesterday he was playing. (4)

3 The pupils are now working; yesterday they were not working. (6)

4 Today we are fighting well; yesterday we were not fighting well. (7)

5 Yesterday I was reading a book; today I am doing nothing. (6)

6 Today the slaves are working quickly, but yesterday they were working slowly. (8)

7 Listen to the teacher, boy! Yesterday you were not listening to the teacher. (7)

8 Fight well, Romans! Yesterday you were not fighting well. (7)

9 Today they are walking, but yesterday they were running. (5)

10 Many slaves were hurrying along the road. (5)

Total: 60

Exercise 16.10

1 The teacher was saying many words. (4)

2 The sailors often used to stay in the villa. (5)

3 Why were you running, boy? (3)

4 I was running beacuse I was afraid. (3)

5 The woman often used to give water to the boys. (5)

6 The Romans were attacking. Today they are not attacking. (5)

7 Many slaves were running out of the town. (5)

8 The girls were playing but the boys were not playing. (6)

9 The Romans often used to fight against the Greeks. (5)

10 The Greeks were not afraid of the Romans. (4)

Total: 45

Exercise 16.11

1 The Romans were attacking the town. (3)

2 The boy was walking to the villa. (4)

3 The teacher was savage. (3)

4 I used to like girls. (2)

5 The poet was reading a book. (3)

6 The slaves were fighting in the fields. (4)

7 The boys were not listening to the teacher. (4)

8 Why were you not working, boys? (4)

9 We were walking along the road. (3)

10 Why were you laughing? (2)

Total: 32

Exercise 16.12

1 I was afraid because the teacher was angry. (5)

2 A great crowd of boys was coming. (4)

3 The boys were not looking at the girls. (4)

4 The slaves were running out of the town. (4)

5 Why was the teacher not praising the girls? (5)

6 The teacher was not praising the girls because the girls were not working. (8)

7 The sailors were often drinking wine. (4)

8 The boy did not like the teacher. (4)

9 Slaves often used to fight in the streets. (5)

10 I was running quickly. (2)

Total: 45

Exercise 16.13

1 amabat.

2 videbamus.

3 regebant.

4 eram.

5 audiebatis.

6 legebamus.

7 currebas.

8 laudabat.

9 ambulabant.

10 mittebam.

1 mark for each question. Total: 10

Exercise 16.14

1 poeta legebat.

2 poetae legebant.

3 Flavia cantabat.

4 puellae cantabant.

5 servus pugnabat.

6 servi pugnabant.

7 Romani oppugnabant.

8 agricolae laborabant.

9 equi bibebant.

10 discipulus spectabat.

2 marks for each question. Total: 20

Exercise 16.15

1 discipulus librum legebat.

2 discipuli magistrum audiebant.

3 agricola scutum portabat.

4 equus aquam bibebat.

5 Graeci Romanos spectabant.

3 marks for each question. Total: 15

Exercise 16.16

1 agricolae murum aedificabant.

2 servus filiam habebat.

3 servus bonus erat.

4 servi boni erant.

5 magister discipulos terrebat.

3 marks for each question. Total: 15

Exercise 16.17

1 You stand.	2nd person	Singular
2 He is present.	3rd person	Singular
3 They want.	3rd person	Plural

4 They are away.	3rd person	Plural
5 He drinks.	3rd person	Singular
6 We build.	1st person	Plural
7 You play.	2nd person	Plural
8 They overcome.	3rd person	Plural
9 He orders.	3rd person	Singular
10 He decides.	3rd person	Singular

3 marks for each question. Total: 30

Exercise 16.18

1 movetis.	You move.
2 iubemus.	We order.
3 adsunt.	They are present.
4 legit.	He reads.
5 navigat.	He sails.
6 iaciebas.	You were throwing.
7 discedebant.	They were departing.
8 oppugnabam.	I was attacking.
9 aberat.	He was away.
10 ludebamus.	We were playing.

2 marks for each question. Total: 20

Exercise 16.19

1 puella sagittam habet.

2 dea reginam monet.

3 regina deam amat.

4 insula viam habet.

5 dea reginam laudat.

6 poeta pecuniam movet.

7 hasta feminam terret.

8 regina puellam vocat.

9 puella reginam videt.

10 nauta aquam spectat.

3 marks for each question. Total: 30

Exercise 16.20

1 amat.	He loves.
2 monemus.	We warn.
3 navigant.	They sail.
4 aedificas.	You build.

5 iubeo.	I order.
6 statis.	You stand.
7 delet.	He destroys.
8 flent.	They cry.
9 damus.	We give.
10 respondet.	He answers.

2 marks for each question. Total: 20

Exercise 16.21

1 maneo.	I stay.
2 ambulas.	You walk.
3 habemus.	We have.
4 cantat.	He sings.
5 monent.	They warn.
6 clamant.	They shout.
7 videt.	He sees.
8 spectant.	They watch.
9 ridetis.	You laugh.
10 pugnat.	He fights.

2 marks for each question. Total: 20

Exercise 17.1

Orbilius was a teacher.(3) Once upon a time he was working in school.(3) Many pupils were present.(3) Marcus was also present.(3) The pupils were working well.(3) Orbilius therefore was happy.(4)

Suddenly a wasp entered the school.(4) Marcus and his friends heard, then saw the wasp.(6) They were not working now.(3) They were looking at the wasp.(2) Because the pupils were not working,(3) Orbilius was very angry.(4) He therefore decided to kill the wasp immediately.(5)

The wasp was now in great danger.(4) It was on the wall.(3) Orbilius saw the wasp.(3) He hurried to the wasp.(3) He killed the wasp.(2) He took the wasp(2) and showed it to the pupils.(3) 'Look!'he shouted to Marcus and his friends.(4) 'I have killed the wasp!(2) Now work, boys!'(3)

Total: 75

Exercise 17.2

1 Subject: **Orbilius**. Object: **vespam**. (2)

2 Accusative. After the preposition **ad**. (2)

3 laborate! (line 14). (1)

Total: 5

Exercise 17.3

1 portavi.

2 spectavistis.

3 navigavit.

4 laboravimus.

5 pugnavit.

6 cantavisti.

7 rogavit.

8 aedificavistis.

9 clamavimus.

10 ambulavit.

11 paraverunt.

12 laudavimus.

13 intravit.

14 navigavit.

15 cantaverunt.

16 laboravit.

17 pugnavimus.

18 oppugnavisti.

19 navigaverunt.

20 intravimus.

1 mark for each question. Total: 20

Exercise 17.4

1 oppugnavimus.

2 paravi.

3 amavit.

4 festinavistis.

5 ambulavit.

6 intravi.

7 necavit.

8 superaverunt.

9 amavimus

10 oppugnaverunt.

11 festinavit.

12 laboraverunt.

13 clamavi.

14 amavimus.

15 aedificavit.

16 vocavistis.

17 intraverunt.

18 habitavimus.

19 vocavisti.

20 pugnaverunt.

1 mark for each question. Total: 20

Exercise 17.5

1 We attacked the town.

2 He entered the temple.

3 They carried the money.

4 I praised the slaves.

5 You built a wall.

6 He killed the messenger.

7 I loved the girl.

8 We killed the horse.

9 He praised the pupils.

10 We built a temple.

2 marks for each question. Total: 20

Exercise 17.6

1 They asked the friends.

2 I watched the girl.

3 You prepared dinner.

4 They built temples.

5 We asked the teacher.

6 They carried shields.

7 He loved wars.

8 They attacked the town.

9 You praised the boy.

10 I killed the master.

2 marks for each question. Total: 20

Exercise 17.7

1 He loved.

2 We sang.

3 You watched.

4 I worked.

5 You called.

6 I sailed.

7 They shouted.

8 He walked.

9 They called.

10 You fought.

11 I killed.

12 We prepared.

13 You praised.

14 We entered.

15 We hurried.

16 You sailed.

17 They prepared.

18 They killed.

19 He praised.

20 They hurried.

21 He carried.

22 You loved.

23 You sang.

24 They worked.

25 I built.

26 He shouted.

27 We walked.

28 He watched.

29 You walked.

30 They sailed.

1 mark for each question. Total: 30

Exercise 17.8

1 You prepared.

2 We called.

3 They praised.

4 He hurried.

5 They built.

6 He prepared.

7 They watched.

8 We carried.

9 You called.

10 He sailed.

11 He worked.

12 He sang.

13 They loved.

14 I carried.

15 I shouted.

16 He fought.

17 He built.

18 They attacked.

19 I watched.

20 You entered.

21 You built.

22 They fought.

23 He lived.

24 He called.

25 I walked.

26 You hurried.

27 We praised.

28 They entered.

29 You carried.

30 He killed.

1 mark for each question. Total: 30

Exercise 17.9

1 The master praised the slave.
2 The master praised the slaves.
3 The Romans attacked the town.
4 The Romans built many towns.
5 The slave prepared dinner.
6 The Romans overcame the Greeks.
7 The sailor built a wall.
8 The messenger watched the battle.
9 The slaves loved the master.
10 The farmer carried the girl.
11 The girl looked at the temple.
12 The boy asked for help.
13 The woman prepared a good dinner.
14 The farmer looked at the girl.
15 The Romans attacked the walls.
16 The Romans built walls.
17 The Greeks carried shields.
18 The inhabitants overcame the Romans.
19 The man entered the villa.
20 The arrow killed the man.

3 marks for each question. Total: 60

Exercise 17.10

1 monuimus.
2 terruisti.
3 habuit.
4 tenuerunt.
5 terrui.
6 timui.
7 tenuit.
8 tenuit.
9 habuerunt.
10 terruistis.
11 timuimus.
12 timuimus.
13 habuimus.
14 habuisti.
15 monuit.
16 timuerunt.
17 habuimus.
18 monuisti.
19 tenui.
20 timuit.

1 mark for each question. Total: 20

Exercise 17.11

1 servus amicum habet.
2 amicus servum amat.
3 ventus puerum terret.
4 puer ventum timet.
5 dominus nuntium iubet.
6 nuntius dominum necat.
7 deus aurum amat.
8 puer periculum timet.
9 periculum puerum terret.
10 equus cibum amat.

3 marks for each question. Total: 30

Exercise 17.12

1	amo.	I love.
2	monet.	He warns.
3	paramus.	We prepare.
4	habes.	You have.
5	tenemus.	We hold.
6	navigat.	He sails.
7	terrent.	They frighten.
8	portant.	They carry.
9	spectatis.	You watch.
10	times.	You fear.

2 marks for each question. Total: 20

Exercise 18.1

Once upon a time Flavia wanted to prepare dinner in her villa.(6) Marcus used to love Flavia's dinners.(4) However, Flavia did not have much food in the villa.(4) She therefore decided to go into town and to buy some food there.(8) And so she went out of the villa(4) and walked along the street to the town.(6)

In the street was a pub.(4) When Flavia came to the pub,(4) she decided to enter and buy some wine.(5) However, when she entered the pub(4) she saw a dreadful sight.(3) She saw Marcus.(2) He was kissing a girl!(3) When Marcus saw Flavia(4) he immediately blushed.(2) 'Marcus!' shouted Flavia.(3) 'What are you doing?'(2) 'I'm doing nothing,'(2) replied Marcus.(2) 'This is Valeria.(3) Valeria is my new girlfriend.'(4) 'You are a dreadful boy, Marcus,'(4) said Flavia.(2) 'I hate you.'(2) She ran out of the pub crying(4) and hurried towards the villa.(4) She was angry.(2) She was very angry.(3)

Total: 100

Exercise 18.2

1 (i) cupiebat (line 1); amabat (line 2); habebat (line 3); erat (lines 6/15/16); basiabat (line 9)   (1)

   (ii) constituit (lines 4/7); exiit (line 5);ambulavit (line 5); venit (line 7); intravit (line 8); vidit (lines 9/10); rubuit (line 10); clamavit (line 11); respondit (line 12); cucurrit (line 15)   (1)

   (iii) facis (line 11); facio (line 12); est (lines 12/13); es (line 14)   (1)

   (iv) parare (line 1); ire (line 4); emere (lines 4/7); intrare (line 7)   (1)

2 3rd. Singular. sum. (There) was.   (4)

3 puer means 'boy' and puerile means boyish or childish.   (2)

4 Ablative. After the preposition e.   (2)

Total: 12

Exercise 18.3

1 reximus.   6 rexerunt.

2 dixisti.   7 duxistis.

3 duxit.   8 dixit.

4 dixi.   9 duxi.

5 dixerunt.   10 diximus.

1 mark for each question. Total: 10

Chapter 18

Exercise 18.4

1 audiverunt.

2 dormivisti.

3 audivi.

4 puniverunt.

5 dormivit.

6 dormiverunt.

7 dormivit.

8 punivit.

9 punivimus.

10 audivistis.

1 mark for each question. Total: 10

Exercise 18.5

1	servi fessi	tired slaves
2	puellae bonae	good girls
3	feminae perterritae	frightened women
4	templa nova	new temples
5	agricolae irati	angry farmers

2+2 marks for each question. Total: 20

Exercise 18.6

1	puella pulchra	a beautiful girl
2	servus validus	the strong slave
3	bellum malum	a bad war
4	puer malus	a bad boy
5	nauta bonus	a good sailor

2+2 marks for each question. Total: 20

Exercise 18.7

1	habent.	They have.
2	ambulabatis.	You were walking.
3	amavistis.	You loved.
4	rexerunt.	They ruled.
5	festinabamus.	We were hurrying.

2+2 marks for each question. Total: 20

Exercise 18.8

1	currit.	He runs.
2	timebat.	He was afraid.

3 audivit.   He heard.

4 audit.   He hears.

5 monuit.   He warned.

2 marks for each question. Total: 10

Exercise 18.9

1 discipuli magistros audiverunt.   The pupils listened to the teachers.

2 nautae oppida oppugnaverunt.   The sailors attacked the towns.

3 puellae pueros amaverunt.   The girls loved the boys.

4 domini servos puniverunt.   The masters punished the slaves.

5 pueri ad villas ambulabant.   The boys were walking to the villas.

3+3 marks for each question. Total: 30

Exercise 18.10

1 servus dormivit.   The slave slept.   (2+2)

2 servus librum portavit.   The slave carried a book.   (3+3)

3 ancilla cenam parabat.   The maidservant was preparing dinner.   (3+3)

4 discipulus in oppidum currit.   The pupil is running into the town.   (3+3)

5 magister verbum malum dixit.   The teacher said a wicked word.   (4+4)

Total: 30

Exercise 18.11

1 nuntius equum habet.   6 servus agrum habet.

2 servus murum aedificat.   7 dominus servum laudat.

3 deus templum amat.   8 servus vinum amat.

4 ventus oppidum delet.   9 puer proelium timet.

5 ager cibum dat.   10 equus dominum amat.

3 marks for each question. Total: 30

Exercise 19.1

1 rexistis.
2 duxi.
3 dormivimus.
4 clamavimus.
5 terruisti.
6 terruit.
7 rexerunt.
8 clamavit.
9 dormivisti.
10 clamavistis.

11 dormivi.
12 clamavi.
13 terruistis.
14 portavit.
15 rexisti.
16 habuisti.
17 audivimus.
18 dormivistis.
19 monui.
20 festinavistis.

1 mark for each question. Total: 20

Exercise 19.2

1 portaverunt.
2 portavistis.
3 terruerunt.
4 rexi.
5 duximus.
6 portavisti.
7 spectaverunt.
8 terrui.
9 festinavit.
10 spectavi.

11 audivi.
12 monuerunt.
13 punivimus.
14 festinaverunt.
15 timuistis.
16 timuisti.
17 diximus.
18 clamaverunt.
19 festinavisti.
20 audivisti.

1 mark for each question. Total: 20

Exercise 19.3

1 We had.
2 They held.

3 I fought.
4 He said.

5 He led.

6 You slept.

7 We led.

8 They ruled.

9 They frightened.

10 You feared.

11 I worked.

12 You warned.

13 I had.

14 You led.

15 He slept.

16 We ruled.

17 You punished.

18 We said.

19 I was.

20 We hurried.

1 mark for each question. Total: 20

Exercise 19.4

1 The pupils slept.

2 We heard the words.

3 You punished the slave.

4 I ruled the land.

5 We feared the goddess.

6 The teachers were good.

7 We attacked the town.

8 I praised the pupil.

9 You held the swords.

10 The pupils feared.

2 marks for each question. Total: 20

Exercise 19.5

1 The sailors attacked the town.

2 The pupil feared the master.

3 The slave led the horse.

4 He said many words.

5 The master punished the slaves.

6 The boys praised the slave.

7 The pupils listened to the messenger.

8 The teacher frightened the pupils.

9 The boy held a sword.

10 The slaves led the horses.

3 marks for each question. Total: 30

Exercise 19.6

1 dedit.

2 duxerunt.

3 dormivi.

4 fecisti.

5 fugerunt.

6 dixit.

7 cucurrerunt.

8 stetistis.

9 mansit.

10 duxit.

11 dormivimus.

12 fecistis.

13 fecerunt.

14 duximus.

15 dixi.

16 mansisti.

Chapter 19

17 dedi.

18 fecit.

19 viderunt.

20 dixistis.

21 feci.

22 audivit.

23 steterunt.

24 fuerunt.

25 stetit.

26 cucurrimus.

27 fugisti.

28 mansistis.

29 fecimus.

30 vidisti.

1 mark for each question. Total: 30

Exercise 19.7

1 cucurri.

2 vidimus.

3 delevit.

4 deleverunt.

5 dixerunt.

6 dederunt.

7 stetisti.

8 mansimus.

9 dormivit.

10 fugit.

11 vidi.

12 duxisti.

13 manserunt.

14 fugimus.

15 delevi.

16 vidit.

17 delevistis.

18 cucurrit.

19 dedimus.

20 dormiverunt.

21 moverunt.

22 venimus.

23 iussit.

24 scripserunt.

25 misisti.

26 responderunt.

27 iecerunt.

28 risistis.

29 posuit.

30 ostendi.

1 mark for each question. Total: 30

Exercise 19.8

1 venit.

2 cupivit.

3 consumpsit.

4 discesserunt.

5 cepit.

6 constituit.

7 luserunt.

8 biberunt.

9 posuerunt.

10 bibisti.

11 lusimus.

12 monuistis.

13 cupivimus.

14 discessit.

15 lusi.

16 consumpsistis.

17 cepi.

18 scripsit.

19 constituerunt.

20 venerunt.

21 bibit.

22 consumpsimus.

23 legit.

24 veni.

25 cupiverunt.

26 misit.

27 cepistis.

28 ieci.

29 constituimus.

30 scripsimus.

1 mark for each question. Total: 30

Exercise 19.9

1 servus gladium habet.

2 servus gladium tenet.

3 dominus/magister periculum videt.

4 nuntius vinum portat.

5 gladius puerum necat.

6 ventus murum delet.

7 magister/dominus puerum monet.

8 puer magistrum/dominum timet.

9 servus templum spectat.

10 deus caelum spectat.

3 marks for each question. Total: 30

Exercise 19.10

1 iubeo.   I order.

2 stat.   He stands.

3 flet.   He cries.

4 manet.   He stays.

5 navigat.   He sails.

6 damus.   We give.

7 stamus.   We stand.

8 respondet.   He answers.

9 clamatis.   You shout.

10 delent.   They destroy.

1+1 marks for each question. Total: 20

Exercise 20.1

Flavia ran out of the pub.(4) She was crying but she was very angry.(5) Marcus and Valeria stayed in the pub.(4) Marcus looked at Valeria.(3) Valeria looked at Marcus.(3) For a long time they said nothing.(4) At last Valeria asked Marcus:(3) 'Who was that girl, Marcus?'(5) Marcus replied:(2) 'That girl was Flavia.(4) She is ... was ... my girlfriend.'(4)

'Your girlfriend?!'(2) shouted Valeria.(2) She was angry.(2) 'You have two girlfriends, Marcus?(4) Both Flavia and me?(3) Answer, Marcus!(2) Answer, immediately!(2) I am angry.'(2)

Marcus however did not want to reply to Valeria.(6) He blushed again.(2)

'I do not love you, Marcus,' said Valeria.(6) 'You are a wicked boy.(3) You are not my friend.(5) Goodbye!'(1) When she said these words,(4) she thumped Marcus(2) and angrily hurried out of the pub.(5)

Marcus remained in the pub, amazed.(4) He was alone.(2)

Total: 100

Exercise 20.2

1 (i) cucurrit (line 1)/manserunt (line 3)/spectavit (line 4)/rogavit (line 5)/
respondit (line 7)/clamavit (line 9)/cupivit (line 13)/rubuit (line 13)/
dixit (line 16)/pulsavit (line 16)/festinavit (line 17). (1)

  (ii) flebat (line 1); erat (lines 2/6/7/8/19). (1)

  (iii) responde (line 11). (1)

  (iv) respondere (line 12). (1)

2 3rd. Plural. maneo. (3)

3 Masculine. (1)

4 Ablative. After the preposition e. (2)

Total: 10

Exercise 20.3

1 I gave.

2 He departed.

3 You sent.

4 You destroyed.

5 You laughed.

6 We ordered.

7 You ran.

8 You did.

9 They stayed.

10 He was.

11 He took.

12 He heard.

13 I did.

14 He ruled.

15 He threw.

16 He answered.

17 We were.

18 You gave.

19 They did.

20 We stayed.

21 We stood.

22 We did.

23 You saw.

24 They gave.

25 They drank.

26 I came.

27 We destroyed.

28 They played.

29 You drank.

30 They said.

1 mark for each question. Total: 30

Exercise 20.4

1 They sent.

2 They laughed.

3 They departed.

4 He ordered.

5 He said.

6 They wrote.

7 I saw.

8 They took.

9 They destroyed.

10 You did.

11 He gave.

12 I ordered.

13 I ran.

14 He stood.

15 You ordered.

16 He did.

17 I said.

18 He sent.

19 He laughed.

20 We departed.

21 He ran.

22 They ordered.

23 He put.

24 He saw.

25 They stood.

26 I answered.

27 They ran.

28 We gave.

29 He stayed.

30 We saw.

1 mark for each question. Total: 30

Exercise 20.5

1 The man stood.

2 The horse ran.

3 The girls stayed.

4 Help came.

5 The slaves slept.

6 The teacher answered.

7 The Romans fled.

8 The sailors departed.

9 The queen laughed.

10 The master decided.

2 marks for each question. Total: 20

Exercise 20.6

1 I read the books.

2 You led the horse.

3 I wrote a book.

4 He took the shield.

5 I threw a spear.

6 He saw the queen.

7 We drank wine.

8 They moved the wall.

9 You ate the food.

10 They destroyed the temples.

2 marks for each question. Total: 20

Exercise 20.7

1 vir bibit.

2 puella dormivit.

3 Romani venerunt.

4 nauta legit.

5 discipuli riserunt.

6 servus fugit.

7 socii discesserunt.

8 puer respondit.

9 amici manserunt.

10 nuntius cucurrit.

2 marks for each question. Total: 20

Exercise 20.8

1 scutum tenui.

2 puellam amaverunt.

3 librum legimus.

4 oppidum oppugnavit.

5 locum vidisti.

6 villas deleverunt.

7 aquam biberunt.

8 cibum misimus.

9 pecuniam cepi.

10 iratus fui.

2 marks for each question. Total: 20

Exercise 20.9

1 magister/dominus librum scripsit.

2 servi cibum moverunt.

3 Graeci villam deleverunt.

4 discipulus aquam iecit.

5 nautae oppidum ceperunt.

3 marks for each question. Total: 15

Exercise 20.10

1 amici e templo cucurrerunt. (4)

2 femina librum pueris legit. (4)

3 nauta vinum bibere constituit. (4)

4 Romani murum in proelio deleverunt. (5)

5 agricolae equum ex agro duxerunt. (5)

Total: 22

Exercise 20.11

1 The sailor sailed from the island. (4)

2 The girls slept well. (3)

3 The teacher wrote a good book. (4)

4 We heard the queen. (2)

5 The slaves fled out of the town. (4)

6 The small boy ran into the road. (5)

7 The boy stood on the wall. (3)

8 What did you do, boys? (3)

9 The man threw a spear. (3)

10 We quickly came to the town. (4)

Total: 35

Exercise 20.12

1 You have not read the book, pupils. (4)

2 The maidservants drank water and wine. (5)

3 Many slaves worked in the villa. (5)

4 The master gave much money to the slave. (5)

5 The teacher ordered the pupils to work. (4)

6 The Romans decided to attack the wall. (4)

7 The man took the sword and ran into battle. (7)

8 The Greeks threw many spears at the Romans. (6)

9 The pupils did not hear the words of the teacher. (5)

10 The slave led the horses out of the fields. (5)

Total: 50

Exercise 20.13

1 I sent a good book to a friend. (5)

2 The master said many words to the slaves. (5)

3 Valeria asked Marcus: 'Why did you not answer?' (6)

4 I decided to be good. (3)

5 The boys played with friends in the road. (6)

6 The danger frightened the sailors. (3)

7 We showed gold to the master. (3)

8 The slave wanted to take the money. (4)

9 We put the money in the temple of the gods. (5)

10 The Greeks did not flee from danger. (5)

Total: 45

Exercise 20.14

1 agricola equum habet.

2 femina servum habet.

3 puella dominum/magistrum amat.

4 dominus/magister puellam amat.

5 periculum ancillam terret.

6 ancilla periculum timet.

7 nauta gladium spectat.

8 regina gladium tenet.

9 gladius filiam necat.

10 poeta vinum amat.

3 marks for each question. Total: 30

Exercise 21.1

1 We run.

2 We were running.

3 We ran.

4 I fought.

5 I was fighting.

6 I fight.

7 They were seeing.

8 They see.

9 They saw.

10 You hear.

11 You heard.

12 You were hearing.

13 He is.

14 He was.

15 He was.

16 You sent.

17 You send.

18 You were sending.

19 I was destroying.

20 I destroyed.

21 I destroy.

22 He writes.

23 He wrote.

24 He was writing.

25 We were giving.

26 We give.

27 We gave.

28 They laugh.

29 They laughed.

30 They were laughing.

1 mark for each question. Total: 30

Exercise 21.2

1 They read.

2 We threw.

3 They were attacking.

4 They built.

5 He ordered.

6 They overcome.

7 They decided.

8 You were moving.

9 We were wanting.

10 We ate.

11 He stood.

12 I drank.

13 They were sitting.

14 He answers.

15 He answered.

16 I asked.

17 I fear.

18 We were frightening.

19 They see.

20 He was entering.

21 They fought.

22 He was working.

23 We shout.

24 They departed.

25 You punish.

26 I wrote.

27 I cry.

28 He gave.

29 They were making.

30 They were.

1 mark for each question. Total: 30

Exercise 21.3

1 cantamus.

2 cantavimus.

3 cantabamus.

4 video.

5 vidi.

6 videbam.

7 cucurrerunt.

8 currebant.

9 currunt.

10 venitis.

11 venistis.

12 veniebatis.

13 sunt.

14 fuerunt.

15 erant.

16 dormiebamus.

17 dormivimus.

18 dormimus.

19 capit.

20 cepit.

21 capiebat.

22 ducebas.

23 duxisti.

24 ducis.

25 deleverunt.

26 delent.

27 delebant.

28 stabam.

29 sto.

30 steti.

1 mark for each question. Total: 30

Exercise 21.4

1 erat.

2 videmus.

3 vidimus.

4 scribis.

5 scripsisti.

6 venit.

7 veniebat.

8 sum.

9 ducebat.

10 mittunt.

11 dabam.

12 venerunt.

13 vocavit.

14 necabamus.

15 ridebamus.

16 riserunt.

17 constituebam.

18 constitui.

19 oppugnamus.

20 iaciebant.

21 navigabatis.

22 monet.

23 consumebant.

24 discessimus.

25 ducunt.

26 miserunt.

27 regebamus.

28 rogo.

29 festinavistis.

30 laudabant.

1 mark for each question. Total: 30

Exercise 21.5

1 amat.   He loves.

2 scripsistis.   You wrote.

3 laudabamus.   We were praising.

4 iecerunt.   They threw.

5 oppugnabas.   You were attacking.

6 navigo.   I sail.

7 constituebat.   He was deciding.

8 moverunt.   They moved.

9 cupitis.   You want.

10 stabamus.   We were standing.

2 marks for each question. Total: 20

Exercise 21.6

1 bibo.   I drink.

2 aderat.   He was present.

3 legerunt.   They read.

4 discessisti.   You departed.

5 delebatis.   You were destroying.

6 puniebamus.   We were punishing.

7 fleo.   I cry.

8 scripsisti.   You wrote.

9 dormiverunt.   They slept.

10 mittebamus.   We were sending.

2 marks for each question. Total: 20

Exercise 21.7

1	cantat.	He sings.
2	ducebam.	I was leading.
3	venimus.	We came.
4	audivistis.	You heard.
5	intrabatis.	You were entering.
6	respondet.	He answers.
7	rogabatis.	You were asking.
8	timebamus.	We were afraid.
9	habuisti.	You had.
10	posuit.	He put.

2 marks for each question. Total: 20

Exercise 21.8

1	They threw.	iacio.
2	They were attacking.	oppugno.
3	You sail.	navigo.
4	We build.	aedifico.
5	He ordered.	iubeo.
6	They were overcoming.	supero.
7	I was moving.	moveo.
8	He decides/decided.	constituo.
9	We wanted.	cupio.
10	They stand.	sto.

2 marks for each question. Total: 20

Exercise 21.9

1	They drank.	bibo.
2	He eats.	consumo.
3	I read.	lego.
4	You departed.	discedo.
5	You ordered.	iubeo.
6	He was away.	absum.
7	He is present.	adsum.

8 They destroyed.   deleo.

9 They punish.   punio.

10 I was writing.   scribo.

2 marks for each question. Total: 20

Exercise 21.10

1 You give.   do.

2 You show.   ostendo.

3 We were sleeping.   dormio.

4 I came.   venio.

5 We hear.   audio.

6 You ran.   curro.

7 He ruled.   rego.

8 We were sending.   mitto.

9 He said.   dico.

10 You were sitting.   sedeo.

2 marks for each question. Total: 20

Exercise 21.11

1 servus aquam portat.   6 regina nuntium iubet.

2 vir murum delet.   7 nuntius filiam habet.

3 nuntius reginam laudat.   8 turba templum aedificat.

4 regina servum vocat.   9 deus pecuniam dat.

5 servus reginam amat.   10 dea deum amat.

3 marks for each question. Total: 30

Exercise 21.12

1 puer proelium timet.   6 hasta virum terret.

2 proelium puerum terret.   7 unda murum delet.

3 nauta reginam monet.   8 turba templum oppugnat.

4 nuntius oppidum intrat.   9 filius gladium habet.

5 turba caelum spectat.   10 poeta librum videt.

3 marks for each question. Total: 30

Exercise 21.13

1 festinant.	They hurry.
2 monetis.	You warn.
3 timet.	He fears.
4 dant.	They give.
5 amamus.	We love.
6 clamat.	He shouts.
7 delemus.	We destroy.
8 terremus.	We frighten.
9 portas.	You carry.
10 videmus.	We see.

2 marks for each question. Total: 20

Test exercises

Test 1

1 She is a Roman girl. (2)

2 In a villa. (1)

3 Aurelia likes Valeria. She invites Valeria to dinner. Dinner is good. The girls are happy. They laugh. (10)

4 Subject: **Aurelia**. Object: **Valerium**. (2)

Total: 15

Test 2

1 A lot of money and many slaves. (2)

2 In the fields. (1)

3 They are afraid of him. (1)

4 Gaius is a slave. He is a lazy slave. He never works in Valerius' fields. Gaius does not like Valerius. Valerius does not like Gaius. Valerius often punishes Gaius because he never works in the fields. (15)

5 **sum.** (1)

6 Genitive. (1)

7 3rd. Singular. (2)

8 Ablative. After the preposition **in**. (2)

Total: 25

Test 3

1 A teacher. (1)

2 Many. (1)

3 They are good and always work. (2)

4 He is happy. (1)

5 One of the pupils however, Publius, never works. He never listens to Orbilius' words. He is always playing in school. When Orbilius sees Publius, he is angry. 'Work immediately, boy!' he shouts. (15)

6 Neuter. (1)

7 verba. (1)

8 perterritus. (1)

9 3rd. Singular. (2)

Total: 25

Test 4

1 He was well known and famous. (2)

2 Capture Britain. (2)

3 Sailed across the sea to Britain. (2)

4 When the Romans came to Britain, they fought against the inhabitants. The inhabitants fought well. The Romans also fought well. However they were not able to overcome the inhabitants of Britain immediately. (15)

5 Adjective: laetus. Infinitive: discedere. (2)

6 Imperfect. sum. (2)

7 Ablative. After the preposition e. (2)

8 3rd. Singular. Perfect. (3)

Total: 30

Test 5

1 A long time. (1)

2 They were angry. (1)

3 Because they were not able to capture Troy. (2)

4 Therefore Ulysses, a famous Greek, ordered his friends to build a big horse. When the Greeks made the horse they put it near the town of Troy. Then they departed. The Trojans led the horse into the town. (20)

5 capere (line 2)/aedificare (line 4). (1)

6 Ablative. After the preposition de. (2)

7 Perfect. (1)

8 3rd. capio. (2)

Total: 30